THE
CHRISTIAN
PERSUADER

THE CHRISTIAN PERSUADER

The Urgency of Evangelism in Today's World

LEIGHTON FORD

World Wide Publications
Minneapolis, Minnesota

THE CHRISTIAN PERSUADER

by Leighton Ford

World Wide Publications is the publishing division of the Billy Graham Evangelistic Association.

Library of Congress Catalog Card Number: 66-22043

ISBN 0-89066-093-X

Printed in the United States of America

Contents

Foreword by Billy Graham

Preface

1. The Crisis in Urgency 15

2. The Recovery of Urgency 25

3. Total Evangelism: A Strategy for Our Day 41

4. The Overwhelming Minority 49

5. By All Means Save Some 61

6. The Role of Mass Evangelism 75

7. Communicating Christ.......................... 85

8. The Conviction of Sin 96

9. The Place of Decision 107

10. Is Evangelism Relevant? 126

Foreword

A FEW years ago an official of the World Council of Churches stated at a consultation on evangelism in Switzerland that if the World Council of Churches adopted a definition of evangelism, it would split the World Council. However, he stated that evangelism, even without a definition, was the most important task facing the church today. He pointed out that the church is rapidly losing out in the world population explosion.

What the World Council of Churches has found difficult to do, Dr. Leighton Ford has brilliantly done in *The Christian Persuader.* I have read many books on evangelism, but *The Christian Persuader* is by far the most clear and comprehensive explanation of what evangelism is. This book is a "must" for pastors, evangelists, students, and Christian laymen.

There is much confusion in the church today about the motive, the message and the methods of evangelism. Dr. Ford probes deeply into all of these areas. A large segment of the modern church uses the term "evangelism" too loosely, describing work that is not necessarily biblical evangelism. No one would deny that the church has a prominent role to play in combating social injustice, but we are in danger of putting the cart before the horse. Man's problem is not just his environment; it is a spiritual disease called "sin," and the cure for the disease is the Gospel, which is the good news about God's love and his provision through Christ Jesus for salvation to all who will repent and believe.

Some forms of modern evangelism are in danger of being almost totally concerned with material comforts for man rather than the proclamation of the "Good News" which he so desperately needs. In short, we are dangerously near to saying to the prodigal son, "It is not necessary to return to your father and home—we can make you comfortable in the pigpen."

I am convinced that if the church would return to the simple, authoritative and urgent message of the *kerygma*, we could accomplish many things for social justice that can never be accomplished by any other methods, however rational they may appear on the surface. No amount of laws can make a man love his neighbor. Law cannot eradicate racial prejudice. We need, of course, a proper social emphasis in our preaching, and we need laws to implement social justice. But we need the transforming power of Christ to give men the capacity to implement these laws—to properly transfer them from the lawbooks into our hearts. After all, it was by the clear preaching of the *kerygma* that the early church made its converts, and its impact upon the Roman world. It was by the preaching of the Gospel that Wesley and Whitefield started a social revolution that is felt to this day. Whitefield so often preached on the text "Ye must be born again," that the church leaders requested him to change his text. His answer was: "I will when you are born again."

What is the strategy of effective evangelism? Have we outgrown, or have we progressed beyond, New Testament methods? Is evangelism relevant for twentieth-century man, caught up in a thousand pressures the nuclear age imposes upon him? Dr. Ford gives the answer!

It is my prayer that *The Christian Persuader* will be used to bring thousands of clergymen and laymen alike back to biblical evangelism, which I believe is just as relevant today as it was when the apostles proclaimed it in the first century.

—Billy Graham

Preface

THE Christian church today is facing a profound crisis as it seeks to relate its historic message in a world convulsed by revolutions.

Not least is this crisis felt in the realm of evangelism.

Our English word "crisis" comes from the Greek *krisis*, meaning a judgment, a sifting, a dividing. There are many critical areas involved in the church's evangelistic mission over which theologians are deeply divided. What constitutes our urgency? What form should the church's mission take? Can the traditional language of evangelism be heard and understood by modern man? Is personal conversion still relevant? How does traditional evangelism bear on our complex social problems?

This book does not pretend to be either a theology or a manual of evangelism. Rather it is an effort to explore some of these crisis areas from my viewpoint and experience as a practicing evangelist, who has wrestled with the challenge of seeking to present Christ effectively both in personal conversation and mass communication.

The present book has grown from the interaction of practical work in evangelism, reading in this field, and many discussions. In it I have tried to express my growing convictions about evangelism today, and in particular about the urgency, the strategy, the communication, and the relevance of the church's task.

The substance of this book was originally given as lectures at the annual Evangelism Conference at Fuller Theological Seminary, Pasadena, California. The final chapter was delivered at the Founder's Day Convocation of Houghton College, Houghton, New York. Subsequently they have been given in whole or in part at Wycliffe College, University of Toronto; McMaster Divinity School, Hamilton, Ontario; the Canadian Theological Students' Conference, Toronto; and various seminars for ministers and theological students in connection with the work of our crusades.

My warmest thanks must go to Billy Graham and our many colleagues throughout the world who have inspired and taught me so much about evangelism; to those whose contributions I have gratefully acknowledged wherever possible, and others whose thoughts I have digested but whose names I may have forgotten; to Dr. Frank Gaebelein, who read the manuscript and offered many helpful suggestions; to the staff at Harper & Row who have been most helpful in every way; to Miss Anne Wolfenden and Miss Jackie Edwards who assisted so faithfully in the typing and preparation of the manuscript; and especially to my family—my wife and children who have supported me by their Christian affection, and my mother, who first encouraged me to do the work of an evangelist.

I once read a book on evangelism prefaced by the author's statement that with that work he was concluding his ministry as an evangelist and departing for other fields. I should like to record my own conviction that there is no greater task in all the world today than that of evangelism. By God's grace I rededicate myself, so long as he shall lead, to the high calling of evangelist.

—Leighton Ford

Charlotte, North Carolina
September, 1966

CHAPTER 1

The Crisis in Urgency

MY little girl was lost.

The certainty hit me, and I fought to keep panic away, to keep my mind clear as I reviewed the facts.

An hour-and-a-half before, Debbie Jean had walked home from school. Thirty minutes ago, after a brief nap, she had gone out to play in the bright spring sun with her four-year-old brother Sandy. My wife had left me with the children while she went to the store, and for some time I worked in my study upstairs. Then when I called Debbie Jean to come in there was no answer. Sandy told me she had gone back to school. This surprised me—although Sharon School was only a few hundred yards away, across some open fields and backyards, she seldom went there to play and never without permission.

I went to look for her in the schoolyard, but she was not there. My wife drove up as I came back home. A little uneasy, we quickly checked the five other houses on our street; she was not at any of them. A neighbor's child said he had seen her go toward school. The mute lady who lived behind us confirmed by signs that she had indeed gone through her yard. Again I walked to the school, but some children playing there had not seen her.

While my wife checked the shopping center across the street, the principal and I went through the classrooms. There was no sign of her. Now I stood on a little-used dirt road between the rear of the school and our house. I looked at the woods. It was hard to push out of my mind stories I had heard of men picking up little girls. Should we call the police? Or was there any other place she might have gone? I walked up and down the road calling, "Debbie Jean," fearing the silence.

Half-an-hour later our little girl came walking around a corner of the school, smiling. The explanation was simple but hard to take. She had gone to a candy store just beyond the school, met a friend, and gone on to her home a half-mile away.

Later (when the thunder and lightning and tears were over!) I reflected on the incident. During the nearly two hours that Debbie Jean was missing, nothing else mattered. In my study were books to be read, letters to be answered, articles to be written, planning to be done—but it was all forgotten. I could think of only one thing: my girl was lost. I had only one prayer, and I prayed it a thousand times, "O God, help me to find her."

But how often, I asked myself, had I as a Christian minister felt that same terrible urgency about men who were lost from God? I once heard an old preacher say, "If man has a soul, and he has, and if that soul can be won or lost for eternity, and it can, then the most important thing in the world is to bring a man to Jesus Christ." Did I really believe he was right?

The question of urgency in evangelism troubles me today as I look at the Christian church throughout the world. If (to quote Emil Brunner) "the church exists by mission as fire exists by burning," what has happened to the fire?

A man once rose in a meeting and prayed, "Lord, if any spark of revival has been lit in this meeting, we pray that you will water that spark!" One sees the complacency of many churches and Christians, and wonders who watered the spark. And how can the flame of what our fathers used to call "a passion for souls" be rekindled?

One thing is clear: we live in a white-hot world. It will not be won by any "cool" philosophy. The uncommitted generation of the fifties is past. Our students have shown by their response to such challenges as the Peace Corps that they want to be committed and involved. Our generation will heed the call to a high and total commitment. But it demands truth which is on fire, truth with passion, truth which demands a profound dedication.

The ultimate prospects of the Gospel are sure. The winds of secular ideologies can never blow out the Light of the World, though sometimes the flame seems to flicker. But God has not made us responsible for the ultimate triumph of Christ. What he has given us is the task of evangelizing this present generation. And we shall most certainly fail in this task unless the church is gripped by a far more compelling urgency than we now evidence.

We need to recover that daring vision which led John R. Mott at the turn of the century to challenge student volunteers to "the evangelization of the world in this generation." The great apostle to the Islamic world, Samuel Zwemer, once wrote, "Evangelism is a collision of souls. We may measure its effect by an equation: $mv = i$ or mass x velocity = impact." If we let mass stand for the truth of the Gospel, then the impact of our Gospel on the world will be in direct proportion to the velocity—the urgency—with which it is delivered.

Before evangelism is a program, it is a passion—a passion of the heart which issues in saving action. Evangelism is the passion of Moses, "Oh, this people have sinned . . . yet now, if thou wilt forgive their sin—if not, blot me, I pray thee, out of the book which thou hast written." It is the passion of Paul, "Woe is me if I preach not the Gospel." It is the anguished cry of Jesus as he weeps over a doomed city, "Oh, Jerusalem, how oft would I have gathered thee."

Evangelism is the cry of Knox, "Give me Scotland or I die," and of Wesley, "The world is my parish." Evangelism is Henry Martyn landing on the shores of India and crying, "Here let me burn out for God!" It is David Brainerd coughing up blood from his tubercular lungs as he prays in the snow for the Indians. It is George Whitefield crossing the Atlantic thirteen times in a small boat to preach in the American colonies.

Evangelism is the passion that leads the artistocratic Lady Donnithorne of our own generation to enter the forbidden slums of Hong Kong's "Walled City" to bring the healing of the Gospel to the pimps and prostitutes, the dope addicts and gamblers. It is Jim Elliot and his young friends staining the sands of a little river in Ecuador with their blood to reach an obscure band of Auca Indians for Christ. It is Paul Carlson leaving his comfortable practice in California for the Congo, there to die with a rebel bullet through his head.

Evangelism is a cross in the heart of God.

We do not automatically have a concern for evangelism. We do not drift into it, for it is a costly business. It cost God his Son. It cost Jesus gaping wounds, bloody sweat, and mocking laughter. When the four men took their paralyzed friend to Jesus, they had to tear up the roof to get him to the Savior. As a friend of mine colorfully comments, "Someone had to pay for that roof." No one ever comes to Jesus unless someone pays for the roof.

Perhaps that is why we are so easily cooled off by the many influences which are deadening our urgency today.

There is, for one thing, a spreading universalism. A pastor, not noted as a theological conservative, said to me some time ago, "I am becoming troubled as I find that so many of my church people really doubt that Jesus is the only Savior of the world. They really don't believe that people need to believe in him."

Universalism is an ancient heresy, which began in the Garden of Eden when the serpent told Adam and Eve, "You shall not die." It was first taught in the Christian church by Origen (A.D. 185-254) of Alexandria, and was later condemned by the church. But the teaching has periodically reappeared, noticeably in post-Reformation times as a reaction to a strict doctrine of election; and in the nineteenth century, when it was known as "the larger hope" of heathen who had not heard the Gospel.

An implicit universalism, which overlooks the seriousness of sin and doubts the universal saviorhood of Jesus Christ, has been widespread in some church circles for years. Many a professing Christian dislikes the very sound of the word "evangelism." It seems to smack of self-righteousness, to imply an attitude of superiority, to be impelled by a holier-than-thou frame of mind. For such people, in their eagerness to express brotherhood and tolerance in a bitter world, "broadmindedness" is the cardinal virtue; serious religious conviction, which might make embarrassing distinctions, almost a deadly sin. An evangelism which holds that Christ is "the way, the truth, and the life" is distressing to them.

Such easygoing tolerance has contributed to much of the current vague universalism. It does not occur to many people that what they call "tolerance" is really sheer lack of conviction. It is not particularly significant if a man who has no great convictions says he is tolerant. Indeed, tolerance is a virtue only if a man believes something very strongly, yet respects the rights of others to disagree. True Christian tolerance is not playing "footsy" with the truth; it is a recognition that while God has uniquely revealed himself in Jesus Christ, he has also allowed men to disobey and disbelieve.

This older universalism threatened the urgency of evangelism because it assumed, for all practical purposes, that men either did not need saving or would all end up saved anyway. In recent years, there has been a fourth resurgence of universalism, which also threatens evangelistic motivation by assuming that men are already saved. Thus one theologian can exclaim, "This is a saved world!" And another world leader in evangelism can warn, on a speaking tour of American seminaries, "It is a heresy to ask a man to accept Christ."

The so-called "new evangelism" sees the Christian task as simply announcing the Lordship of Christ. It finds its roots in the belief that Christ is the Savior of all men, not only in principle but also in present fact. Strangely enough, some of those who lean toward this position are themselves very serious about evangelism. But the new universalism seems certain to short-circuit the church's evangelistic concern in the long run. Why bother ourselves about a task which is not really necessary, when there are so many important things to do in the world?

A second modern factor deadening to the Christian's evangelistic urgency is a kind of mechanical ecclesiasticism. By this, I mean the tacit assumption that a person who has joined a church organization is by virtue of that fact right with God. When a person unites with a local church, or is confirmed, or makes his personal confession of faith, this outward act ought to be a true indicator of an inward and living faith. But is it necessarily so? Was Samuel Shoemaker not closer to the truth when he wrote, "I am shocked to find how many people in our churches have never anywhere made a decisive Christian commitment. They oozed into church membership on a conventional kind of basis, but no one has ever effectively dealt with them spiritually, or helped them make a Christian decision."[1]

Two recent comments underline the growing concern, both Protestant and Roman Catholic, at this point. Dr. John Mackay, president emeritus of Princeton Theological Seminary, stated in the May 27, 1966, *Christianity Today*, " . . . emphasis upon the church as such, upon formal and loyal church membership, . . . can give rise and does give rise in many ecumenical circles, to an impersonal 'churchianity' and a very nominal Christianity . . . The plain truth is that ecclesiastically and even ecumenically speaking, a person can be a church member without being in any basic sense a Christian. Church membership is becoming a substitute for Christian commitment" (page 21). Similarly, a Roman Catholic lay theologian, Gerald McGuire, is quoted in *Faith at Work*, May-June, 1966, as follows: "Since Vatican II the concept of conversion to Christ has gained momentum until it is widely accepted.

We're out to convert Catholics to Christ. Many Catholics have been law-centered rather than Christ-centered" (page 6).

This has been brought home repeatedly to the writer in the course of worldwide evangelistic ministry. How many young people in their teens come forward to make their decision for Christ and say, "I joined the church when I was twelve (or ten, or fourteen) but it meant little to me. I attended a membership class. All my friends were joining. So I joined. But now for the first time I really see the need of a personal relationship to Christ."

We may be thankful that this experience is far from universal. There are many young people who genuinely commit themselves to Christ when they join a church, and who from that time go on in maturing faith. And certainly every kind of evangelism faces the problem of spurious decisions. But the frequency with which young people say that "joining the church" was meaningless ought to make us think very deeply.

A minister of a major Canadian denomination who acted as a Crusade advisor told me afterward that he was troubled by the teen-age inquirers he interviewed who had joined a church as children but said it meant nothing. He felt that he would have to rethink and reshape his entire program of preparing children for church membership.

Christian education ought to lead to a time of personal spiritual choice. Its goal should be conversion and commitment. But is it? When Christian education becomes a substitute for conversion instead of a guide to it, the result is that our churches are filled with people who, as E. Stanley Jones says, "know about God, but don't know him; are informed about Christ, but are not transformed by him; who know about the moral laws, but are powerless to fulfill them."[2]

Certainly "in Christ, in the church" is true, but can we assume that it is also true to say—"in a church, in Christ"? Does the outward form guarantee the inner reality? It was not true under the old covenant. Jeremiah thundered at those who trusted in the circumcision of their flesh, "Circumcise yourselves to the Lord, and take away the foreskins of your heart, ye men of Judah and inhabitants of Jerusalem . . . " (Jeremiah 4:4).

It was not true of John the Baptist's audience. He warned them, "Bring forth therefore fruits worthy of repentance, and begin not to say within yourselves, We have Abraham to our father: for I say unto you, That God is able of these stones to raise up children unto Abraham" (Luke 3:8).

It was not true of Nicodemus. Jesus told this child of the covenant, " . . . Ye must be born again" (John 3:7). It was not true of the twelve disciples. One of them—the treasurer of Jesus' little church—was a devil, said the Lord! It was not true of the virgins in Jesus' parable. Outwardly they were to all appearances the same—all with wedding dresses, all with lamps. But five lacked oil in their lamps.

It was not true of the Pharisees. "Woe unto you," said Jesus, " . . . for you are like unto whited sepulchres, which indeed appear beautiful outward, but are within full of dead men's bones, and of all uncleanness . . . so you also outwardly appear righteous to men, but within you are full of hypocrisy and iniquity" (Matthew 23:27,28).

It was not true of Simon Magus. Peter said to this baptized, professing believer, " . . . thy heart is not right in the sight of God" (Acts 8:21).

We must especially beware, in these days when we bow down at the shrine of statistics, that we do not let the form of religion dull our concern for spiritual reality. Whitefield preached over and over, "You must be born again." This was the note that set the church on fire in England two hundred years ago. It is sorely needed again today.

There is a third deadening factor today—a distorted Calvinism. The doctrine of the sovereignty of God is a shining biblical truth, which at its best compels us to evangelize to the glory of our divine King. But any doctrine can be wrenched and deformed. The "neo-Puritan" movement, especially influential in England, has been a healthy corrective to some of our religious humanism. But we must beware lest the biblical basis of God's sovereignty be divorced from the biblical teaching of man's responsibility, so that Calvinism is distorted into a kind of fatalism.

When Spurgeon was once asked to reconcile these two truths, he replied, "I wouldn't try. I never reconcile friends."

There are some small churches in America which have taken this obsession with one side of the truth to such an extreme that they refuse to have Sunday Schools or to engage in world missions. To do so, they hold, would be to infringe upon God's sovereign rights with human effort! William Carey met this type of thinking two centuries ago. He rose at a ministers' fraternal to propose that they form a missionary society. "Sit down, young man," objected

the chairman. "When God is pleased to convert the heathen, he
will do it without your aid or mine!"

The theme song of this party appears to be:

> Sit down, oh man of God,
> The kingdom he will bring
> Just how and when and where he wilt;
> You cannot do a thing.

At the opposite end of the spectrum is another tendency which
cuts the evangelistic nerve. This I would call a man-centered activism. Some time ago a radio quartet was heard to sing, "Let's
Turn the Tide for God." I am sure God's anxieties were greatly
relieved by this encouragement! What a pitiful picture this presents
of a feeble, frustrated deity, wringing his hands over the mess the
world is in and wondering how he will ever work things out unless
some strong man lends a helping hand!

Where is the living God of Scripture in the scheme—the Lord
God omnipotent who sits in the heavens and laughs at man's preten-
sions of revolt (Psalm 2:4); the Holy One who sits upon the circle
of the earth, and the inhabitants thereof are as grasshoppers (Isaiah
40:22); the God and Father of our Lord Jesus Christ who
" . . . worketh all things after the counsel of his own will" (Ephesians 1:11)?

Make no mistake. Evangelism may be increasingly difficult
in the decades ahead, and that is why "activistic" evangelism will
fail. It is centered on man instead of God. It overstresses human
responsibility and feels the pressure to produce results. Its "success psychology" demands more and better techniques. But when
the best methods meet the hard resistance of stubborn sin, activistic
evangelism is frustrated and retreats into the ghetto of cynicism.

There is one other factor which deadens our sense of urgency. For want of a more accurate description we may call this an
eccentric evangelicalism—an evangelicalism which is centered on
anything except the Lord himself. It would be pleasant to believe
that a correct, conservative, evangelical theology guarantees
evangelistic zeal. But the evidence is not there. True, an evangelical
mind joined with an evangelical heart has produced the greatest
missionaries and evangelists. But a cold heart can beat close to
a correct mind. There are too many churches with impeccable
credentials for orthodox theology whose outreach is almost nil.

They are "sound," but they are sound asleep.

The concern of the New Testament fellowship to penetrate the world around with the Good News is lacking. They are more like a smug and complacent club, whose members are ready to compliment each other on their theological correctness, but who are really in full retreat from the hard job of relevant evangelism. Their orthodox theology has become a way to escape from engagement with a Christless world.

Their trouble is spiritual eccentricity, in a quite literal sense. The secondary has become primary. How sadly Paul commented, " . . . all seek their own, not the things which are Jesus Christ's" (Philippians 2:21). Something other than our Lord may become the focus of attention and the excuse for self-seeking: a theological system, the personality of a leader, an issue in church politics, even a program of evangelism. A Latin Christian observed that North American churches are "mission-centered" rather than "witness-centered." Absorbed in supporting missionaries overseas, they become irrelevant in their witness at home. Is it possible that a church's missionary program could become an idol to the detriment of evangelistic zeal? I am convinced that the Devil can also use church controversies to divert us from our mission. The defense of the "faith once delivered" has a place—but not the central place.

Evangelical eccentricity will deaden our evangelism whenever we forget God's will: " . . . that in all things he [God's dear Son] might have the pre-eminence. For it pleased the Father that in him should all fulness dwell" (Colossians 1:18,19).

A missionary acquaintance of mine was working in Indochina shortly before the fall of Dien Bien Phu. He was taken captive by a band of Communist guerrillas and held for several weeks. During this period he became very friendly with their young officer, and taught him English by means of the Bible.

Toward the end of this time they sat discussing an impending operation in which the guerrillas were going up against tremendous odds. When the missionary pointed out that he might die, the officer thought for a moment and then said quietly, "I would gladly die if I could advance the cause of Communism one more mile." Then he made this telling comment, "You know, as you have read to me from the Bible I have come to believe that you Christians have a greater message than that of Communism. But I believe that we are going to win the world, for Christianity means something to you, but Communism means everything to us."

Such dedication should strike us to the heart. While the emissaries of big business, the missionaries of Islam and other resurgent religions, and the evangelists of Communism are probing the ends of the earth, how long can we who know Christ hold our peace?

Or is there an antidote for our evangelistic complacency?

[1]Samuel Shoemaker, *How to Become a Christian* (New York: Harper & Row, 1953), p. 71.

[2]E. Stanley Jones, *Conversion* (Nashville: Abingdon Press, 1959), p. 180.

CHAPTER 2

The Recovery of Urgency

BILLY GRAHAM told us that a delegate to the World Council of Churches informed the section on evangelism that we need a new urgency for evangelism. It was no longer enough to rescue men from perishing in eternity. Hell is "out" as our urgency. (To which Dr. Graham wryly commented that he still thought there was something to be said for hell!) What is our urgency derived from: a desire to oppose Communism? To preserve the church? To depopulate hell?

Inadequate motives result in an evangelism that is eccentric, artificial, and abortive. Our starting point must be what stands out in the New Testament: the authority of Jesus Christ.

James Denney once entertained in his home a Scottish missionary on furlough from India. The man came in discouraged at night from a church where he had presented the cause of missions. "Denney," he said, "I am ready to give up. I have been pouring out my life in India, and I come home to find that people who are supposed to support us don't care. I don't think they even believe in missions." And Denney flashed back, "Then they have no right to believe in missions, for they do not believe in Jesus Christ!"

Jesus Christ is the urgency of evangelism! Nowhere is this more grippingly apparent than in the life of Paul. Here was a Christ-mastered, Christ-intoxicated man, who has left us the great manifesto of missionary motivation in 2 Corinthians 5:10-21. Here Paul indicates that the secret of his passion lay in three realms.

In each, Jesus Christ was supreme.

There is the realm of theology—the Christ-centered mind. These verses are full of profound theological phrases—"the judgment seat of Christ," "the terror of the Lord," "one died for all," "God was in Christ," "not imputing their trespasses," "the word of reconciliation," "the righteousness of God." Obviously, Paul's passion for souls was not merely an emotion. It was deeply thought out.

Evangelistic urgency cannot be long sustained on emotional appeals. Nor can biblical evangelism endure long when it is grafted to an unbiblical theology. Evangelism and theology belong together. They are partners, not competitors. As Denney said in his fine sentence, "If theologians were our evangelists, and evangelists our theologians, we would have the ideal church."

The evangelical revival of the eighteenth century provides a classical example of theology's relation to evangelism. In the early part of that century the orthodox scholars had met and mastered the assault of the deists. Their victory was largely in the realm of intellectual debate, but it did not lack practical significance. The truth of the Christian faith had been established at the scholarly level before Wesley and Whitefield came along. A highway along which the evangelical revival could move had been built.

Canon Overton showed how unfortunate it was that there should have been any antagonism between the theologians and evangelists of that era. Their competition was needless, for they were working for the same cause and neither could have done the other's part of the work, "Warburton could have no more moved the hearts of living masses, as Whitefield did, than Whitefield could have written *The Divine Legation*. Butler could no more have carried on the great crusade against sin and Satan which Wesley did, than Wesley could have written *The Analogy*. But without such work as Wesley and Whitefield did, Butler's and Warburton's would have been comparatively inefficacious; and without such work as Butler and Warburton did, Wesley's and Whitefield's work would have been, humanly speaking, impossible."[1]

So, today, the church cannot evangelize unless she is certain of her evangel. Dr. Elmer Homrighausen, former Dean of Princeton Seminary, notes that "a decline in evangelistic zeal is always the result of a loss of dynamic faith in the Gospel."

For Paul, the cardinal doctrines of an evangelistic theology were summed up in two phrases: "For we must all appear before the judgment seat of Christ . . . For the love of Christ constraineth us . . . " (2 Corinthians 5:10,14). These tell us something about man: that man is a sinner who stands condemned under the judgment of God, but that man can also be redeemed by the love of God, which acted in the death of Jesus Christ for our reconciliation.

Evangelistic theology must always keep in tension these two poles of the doctrine of man. We must remember, as Denney said, that "the effects of sin on human nature, and especially on the human will must be such that man needs a redeemer; on the other hand, it must only be such that he remains susceptible of redemption."

In recent days we have been told that we must no longer appeal to man as a sinner in need of salvation. Man, say the disciples of Dietrich Bonhoeffer's later writings, has "come of age." The Gospel message must be adjusted to appeal to "modern man," who is self-assured and no longer needs the tutelage of God, let alone to be reconciled to him.

The evangelist must not try to minimize man's achievements in order to make a case for the Gospel. After all, the God who gave us the Gospel also gave man the gifts of science and technology. There is indeed a sense in which man has matured and come of age. The questions that concerned men are asking are real questions, those of adulthood, not babyhood. Most men have outgrown magic; they are no longer interested in superstitious explanations of nature's dark powers; they want to know the way to peace, to social justice, to racial understanding, to economic dignity. They seek a way of personal fulfillment which does not deny the demands of personal integrity.

We cannot and should not deny modern man's improvements over the past. Yet the adult must be measured against the standards we expect of an adult, not those we expect of an adolescent. And measured, not against his grandfather but against his God, twentieth-century man cuts a tragic figure. Has scientific man really "come of age" when he seeks at the same time a way to cure cancer and a way to destroy the world? Huston Smith reported in *Saturday Review* a discussion by scientists at a "Conference on Science and Human Responsibility" at Washington University in St. Louis. They could have no easy faith in progress, he said, because "each step in human advance seems to introduce new problems and perils along with its benefits. We are constantly finding that even where advance is unmistakable it does not result in the elimination or even probable diminution of human ills."[2]

Excellence in education has benefited all mankind. But education has no more brought man to maturity than has science. Theodore Roosevelt once said, "An ignorant bad man may steal from the freight cars on the railroad. If you educate that man without changing his heart, all you're doing is making it possible for him to steal the whole railroad!" The disturbing fact is that the worst wars in history have been fought by the educated, civilized nations.

An African professor of anthropology, Dr. A. K. Busia, writes poignantly of an English journalist who traveled in the Ashanti country of central Ghana in the early nineteenth century. The Englishman witnessed a tribal purification ceremony in which two human sacrifices were led down to a river; knives poked through their cheeks, and sacrificed to their idols. "I was glad that I belonged to a civilized country," was the reaction of the journalist. Dr. Busia says that in 1945 he was studying in Oxford. Browsing in a bookshop one day he idly picked up a pictorial record of the Second World War. As he turned the pages he saw pictures of Dachau, Belsen, and Auschwitz, with the gas ovens, the bleached bones, and the crematoriums.

He bought that book, and also secured a scrapbook. Cutting out a picture of an old tribal chief with his tribal markings, he pasted it in and marked under it "Africa, 1817." On the opposite page he put a picture of the gas ovens at Auschwitz, and under it, with no further comment, wrote "Europe, 1945."

In many ways the twentieth century has been a very cruel and unenlightened piece of history. It is modern man who designed and used the nuclear bomb. It is modern man who finds the way to produce surplus crops in the rich nations, but lets half the world's population go to bed never knowing the luxury of a full stomach. It is modern man who builds superhighways and suffers a constant and bloody carnage on them. It is modern man who is ridden by psychosis and neurosis, who is plagued by juvenile delinquency, who has shamelessly exploited sex, who is torn by the bitterness of racial prejudice, and who tolerates the miseries of drink and gambling. We may well agree with General Omar Bradley's assessment that modern man is "a nuclear giant and an ethical infant."

Without a realistic facing of man's perversity, we fall prey to facile optimism, which seeks to cure man's ills by superficial doses of education, civilization, and scientific progress. But unless we are convinced of man's basic worth, we easily fall into a cynical pessimism like that of Nazism or Communism, which makes man expendable for the good of the state or the class. The biblical doctrine of man is radically realistic, avoiding the Scylla of optimism and the Charybdis of pessimism. In the Scriptures, as Cowper wrote,

> We learn with wonder
> How the world began
> Who made, who marred,
> And who ransomed man.

On the one hand, the New Testament rests on the assumption that men outside of Christ and apart from God are lost and need a Savior. Jesus told his vivid stories of the coin, the sheep, and the son. The common factor was that they were all lost, and that sin is not so much in "badness" as in "awayness." To be lost is to be away—away from the purse, from the sheepfold, and from the father's house. Jesus was teaching the self-righteous Pharisees who condemned him for associating with "sinners" (Luke 15:1,2) that, though they went to the synagogue every Sabbath day, in their hearts they were just as much "lost" and away from God as were the irreligious publicans. Yet the last word is not lost but found. Though man is away from God, he can be brought back; though he is dead in sins, he can be made alive; though he is lost he can be found; and though he is perishing, he can be saved. In God's sight, man in spite of his sin is still of more value than the whole of nature (Matthew 10:31), and to find lost man is worth any pain, any search and any sacrifice on his part.

In a similar vein the apostle Paul recognizes that there is a spiritual blindness by which sin veils the minds and hearts of those who are perishing and keeps them from seeing the truth of the Gospel. Paul himself had once been blind to the beauty of Christ; yet God took the scales from his eyes. So he knew that the same God who caused the light of the first creation to shine into darkness and chaos could perform the miracle of the new creation and flood the hearts of sin-darkened men with light, in the face of Jesus Christ (2 Corinthians 4:3-6). The writer of Hebrews also shows us three pictures of man. There is man as God has made him: " . . . a little lower than the angels, . . . (crowned) with glory and honor, and . . . set . . . over the works of thy hands." There is man as sin has marred him: " . . . We see not yet all things put under him." The crown of creation has become the slave of sin, the

miserable and despairing victim of his own rebellion, without God
and without hope in this world. But there is also the picture of
man as Christ can mend him: " . . . We see Jesus, who was made
a little lower than the angels for the suffering of death, crowned
with glory and honor; that he by the grace of God should taste
death for every man" (Hebrews 2:6-9).

Urgency comes as we share the mind of Christ and his apostles,
who plainly saw man as lost or found, as blind and perishing or
enlightened and saved, as dead in sin or alive in Christ. These
phrases of Paul also tell us something about God: that God is light,
and that God is love. The man who is not deeply convinced of
the holy and righteous wrath of God, the inevitability of judgment—
that it is "appointed unto men once to die and after this the judgment" (Hebrews 9:27)—is not likely to make an effective evangelist.
Tom Allan once told me that he felt the denial of God's judgment
had for years cut the nerve cord of evangelism in Scotland. To many
moderns, that God can punish seems to need explanation.

To the early Christians, that God could forgive was the amazing thing. Can it be that we need again to see the God who is "high
and lifted up," before whom the angels, covering their faces, cry,
"Holy, holy, holy"? Then shall we feel a new urgency to reach
lost and sinful men, facing the judgment of a holy God, and "knowing the terror of the Lord, we [will] persuade men . . . " (2 Corinthians 5:11).

But most deeply, it is the love of Christ that constrains us.
That this God before whom we must appear has so loved men as
to send Jesus to die for them, that he was in Christ reconciling
the world unto himself and not imputing their trespasses unto them,
that he has made him who knew no sin to be sin for us: this is
what compels us to become ministers of the reconciliation.

Two Hindu professors once came to Dr. Emil Brunner and
asked how Christians could say that "in none other is there salvation." He pointed out that the finality of Jesus Christ stemmed from
the fact that he and he alone died for the sins of the world. Neither
Buddha nor Krishna nor Rama died for the sins of mankind. "But
one thing there was not in Indian religion, or in any religion outside Christianity: a man who came on earth to reconcile to God
by the sacrifice of His life those who have become separated from
God by their guilt and sin."[3]

We find evangelistic compulsion in the knowledge that God
"so loved the world." His love was not a vague and sentimental

benevolence. It was a costly and holy love in action. "God commendeth his love toward us, in that, while we were yet sinners, Christ died for us" (Romans 5:8). There is an historical exclusiveness about Jesus Christ. God has spoken a loving Word, but a unique and final Word, in him. This is the "once-for-allness" of the Gospel, the "offence of the cross," the "hard particulars" of the *kerygma*. God sent his Son into the world not to condemn, but to save. But there is a condemnation if men love darkness and reject the light. Our Lord said, "He that honoreth not the Son honoreth not the Father which hath sent him."

P. T. Forsyth once said, "You may always measure the value of Christ's cross by your interest in missions. The missionless church betrays that it is a cross-less church, and it becomes a faithless church."[4]

"Do you really believe what you say, Chaplain?" asked a condemned prisoner of the minister who was trying to bring him to faith in Christ. "If I believed your Gospel were true, I would crawl across England on broken glass to tell men about it." Surely the urgency of our witness will measure the reality of our beliefs.

Paul also found his evangelistic urgency in the realm of experience—the Christ-filled heart. "With us, therefore, worldly standards have ceased to count in our estimate of men . . . When anyone is united to Christ, there is a new world; the old order has gone, and a new order has already begun" (2 Corinthians 5:16a,17, NEB). When the Christ of the judgment seat and the Christ of the cross becomes the Christ of the heart, we cannot help looking at others through new eyes—the eyes of Christ—and sharing with them the one who means so much to us.

The real presence of the living Christ was the authentic first-hand keynote of New Testament evangelism. "Come see a man who told me all things that ever I did," urged the woman of Samaria. "Once I was blind, now I see," was the straightforward testimony of the blind man. "We have found the Messiah," cried Andrew to Peter. And Peter later said, "We cannot help but speak the things which we have seen and heard." An irresistible impulse to share came surging from within.

So it has been through the Christian centuries. Charles Wesley, captive of the grace of the Savior, sang,

> My heart is full of Christ, and longs
> Its glorious matter to declare!

Of him I make my loftier psalms,
I cannot from his praise forbear;
My ready tongue makes haste to sing
The glories of my heavenly King.

It is D. T. Niles, I believe, who beautifully defined evangelism as "one beggar telling another beggar where to find bread." I, a poor beggar, have fed my starving soul on Christ, the Bread of Life—and from the deep satisfaction and strength he has brought, I witness to others of his plenty.

When our witness does not flow from the evangelical experience, we become like the baseball announcer in San Diego who broadcasts descriptions of all games by the local baseball club. If the team is on the road, he gives a play-by-play description from a ticker-tape account of the game fed to him from the other city. Suspended from the ceiling in the studio is a baseball bat. Near the announcer is a leather chair, and by his hand is a cane. When he hits the leather chair with the cane, it sounds exactly like a pitch thumping into the catcher's mitt. When he whacks the bat with the cane, it sounds exactly like the crack of a ball against a bat. The announcer reads the tape—"The pitcher rears back and throws a hard fast one"—Thwack! goes the cane on the chair. "High and outside, ball one!" Again the tape clicks out its message. "Here comes a curve ball—O'Malley swings." Whack! goes the cane against the bat. "It's a long one into right field—it's going—it's going—it's gone!" The announcer turns a knob and the volume comes up on a record of simulated crowd noise. If you are listening to the ball game by radio, you'd vow the announcer was sitting behind home plate at the ball park. There is the brilliant description, the baseball jargon, the sounds of the game. You can almost smell the popcorn! It sounds real; but the announcer is talking about something he has not seen.

It is entirely possible for us to go through a description of the Christian game—with all the brilliant reporting, all the correct sounds, all the Christian jargon—and yet be describing things we have not seen and telling things we have not heard.

What a hollow ring there is to evangelism when it does not overflow from the Christ-filled heart. Then it degenerates into proselytism—an arguing of individuals into a position or a party line, or a recruiting of them into an organization, rather than an introducing of people to a Person. No wonder the world so often mocks and resists our travesty of evangelism. We are like the exorcists, the sons of Sceva in Acts 19, who ordered the devils to come out "in the name of Jesus whom Paul preaches." Note the "Jesus whom Paul preaches." It was not "the Jesus whom we know." They were trying to imitate a performance, not sharing a reality. The demon replied, "Jesus I know, and I am acquainted with Paul, but who on earth are you?" And the man in whom the evil spirit was living sprang at them and overpowered them all with such violence that they rushed out of that house wounded, with their clothes torn off their backs (Acts 19:15,16, Phillips).

Neither should we be surprised if we try to evanglize on the basis of a proxy faith, in the name of the Jesus whom Barth preaches, or Lloyd-Jones, or Graham, or Thielicke, and retreat defeated and wounded. If we cannot say with Paul, "I know whom I have believed," then our first task is to get on our knees with our Bibles and seek Christ until we can.

Two men who have been widely used in effective evangelism testify to the need of personal encounter. The first is a Presbyterian, Dr. H. H. Thompson, who rendered distinguished service as Secretary of Evangelism for the Presbyterian Church, U. S. He tells of an experience in County Antrim, North Ireland, during a year of graduate study. Cycling across the countryside, he stopped to ask information of an old gardener. Before permitting his young guest to depart, the gardener had a question or two for him. "What are you going to do in life, young man?" he asked. Thompson replied that he was looking forward to the ministry and was engaged in special study in Scotland toward that end. The old man immediately followed with another, "Do you know that you yourself are saved?" With what might be called Presbyterian modesty, Thompson recalls, he answered, "I hope I am." Without a moment's hesitation the gardener shot back, "That isn't enough. If you are going to help other people know the Lord, you must be very sure you know Him yourself." And Thompson comments, "I knew the old man was right. Those of us who have not got beyond, 'I hope I am a Christian' will do little for the spiritual welfare of others."[5]

The second is an Episcopalian, the late Samuel Shoemaker, who was used to bring so many into contact with Christ. In his helpful book *How to Become a Christian* he wrote, "The test of a man's conversion is whether he has enough Christianity to get it over to other people. If he hasn't there is something wrong in it." He then related his own failure to get his faith across to others. Shoemaker began lay reading at seventeen, and had a small summer congregation for whom he held services. Several members of that group met tragedy, partly because he was talking about general religion and not personal conversion. "I was like a Scot friend of mine," comments Shoemaker humorously, "who said that while his friends could not make him drunk, he couldn't make them sober!" This recurring pattern of failure to help individuals who were seeking repeated itself while Shoemaker was working in army camps during World War I, and again when he went out to teach at a school in China. But in Peking he was brought up short by a man who challenged him as to whether or not he had ever made a full commitment of his life to Jesus Christ. He held him to this point until he made the commitment, and the very next day the young teacher was able to lead a Chinese businessman to make his decision for Christ. Shoemaker concludes his personal testimony with this pointed challenge: "Test yourself by this: can I get across to other people what I believe about Jesus Christ? If not, what real good am I to them, and what real good am I to Him?"[6]

But how about the servant of God who knows the meaning of commitment to Christ but for whom that warm glow of loyalty to Christ may have faded? Staleness always undercuts urgency. If we are bored with our experience of the Christian life, let's face it honestly. To the question I heard a layman ask, "What has Jesus Christ meant to you since seven o'clock this morning?" we should perhaps answer truthfully, "Not very much at all," and earnestly seek the reason.

This experience of spiritual staleness is not inevitable, but it is so common that we should pause to deal with it thoroughly. We all go through dry periods. But what agony it is to feel that as Christian "pros" we have to hold up the mask of serenity and abounding joy, even when our souls are sucked dry. A friend who was working in the New York Crusade with Billy Graham said that one day the elevator operator in their apartment building remarked, "You people surely are different. You're always pleasant, always smiling, always friendly. Your faith must really mean a lot to you." From that day on, laughed my friend, he and his wife had to put on their widest grin every time they entered the elevator, even though they were snarling inside!

What shall we do with this holy masquerade?

Some would say, "Don't be a hypocrite. If you've got worldly

desires and fleshly thoughts, express them. Go ahead and shock
a few people. The minister is no different than anyone else. You're
a man. If you feel like saying Damn, say it. After all, the thought
is as bad as the act. Didn't Jesus teach that?"

But it is not that easy. Surely this is a perversion of what Jesus
said. If I feel lust, am I then to go on and commit adultery? Or
am I to take the lust to God for cleansing? If I feel anger, am I
to get a gun and commit murder? Or am I to surrender the anger
to God for his healing?

Honesty is not enough. It must be joined to commitment. As
Bruce Larson has pointed out, a worldling may be more honest
about his sins than most Christians. He confides his weakness to
his bartender, his psychiatrist, his friend. He has a minimum of
pretense—but he is equally without power. He has no saving secret.

That is why the committed Christian is not satisfied with just
honesty. We are called not only to be honest about our sins, but
to be saved from them. Honesty without Christ may be just a kind
of twisted phoniness in reverse. Because we are at heart phony,
deceitful people, even so-called honesty may be a cover-up for my
deeper sin of pride—my "God-almightiness."

What, then, should I do about staleness?

1. I should acknowledge it to God and myself. There is no use
playing "let's pretend" with the Searcher of hearts. If I am stale,
he already knows it. If I am going through the old motions without
the old power, like Samson who "wist not that the power had
departed from him" I must admit it—much activity, little fruit.

2. I should take time for a spiritual inventory—a half-day or
a day alone with God and my Bible—allowing him to search my
heart through his Word, to point out any area or act or attitude
of disobedience, of unwillingness to be a servant for Jesus' sake.
When the sin is discovered, the remedy is confession, cleansing,
and new commitment. On the other hand, if I candidly examine
my life in the light of God's Word, and discover no real failure,
I should not go on morbidly seeking to dredge up some sin; rather
I should humbly accept the cleansing God has already given. "To
say that we have not sinned when we have," said A. W. Tozer, "is
to be false to the facts; to insist that we have sinned when we have
not, is to be false to ourselves."[7]

3. I shall probably find genuine help in the fellowship of a
Christian friend, or a group of believers, where there is a fellowship
of openness, prayer, concern, "where committed people can begin

to be honest with one another and discover the dimension of apostolic fellowship." God has seen fit to join together our fellowship with him, and our fellowship with each other. "If we walk in the light as he is in the light, we have fellowship one with another and the blood of Jesus Christ his Son, cleanseth us from all sin" (1 John 1:7).

"If a man say, I love God, and hateth his brother, he is a liar; for he that loveth not his brother whom he hath seen, how can he love God whom he hath not seen?" (1 John 4:20). Spiritual dynamics operate in a triangular relationship with God at the top apex, my neighbor at another, and myself at the third. This is because God's will is not only to reconcile us to himself, but also to each other. Perhaps this is why the Lord allows himself sometimes to seem so much more "real" to us when we are worshiping, praying, and opening our hearts in a group—because he knows our tendency is to overemphasize a kind of abstract love in general in order to avoid loving our brothers in the flesh. However, group confession poses a danger unless it is under the careful discipline of the Word and the Spirit. Again, honesty can become a shibboleth, a subtle means of spiritual dictatorship by which one strong personality in a group manipulates another, and the weaker member feels pressure to confess in order to conform to group expectations. This can be spiritually disastrous. The truly Christian group accepts me as I am, "honest" and "phony," and allows me to respond at the pressure of the Holy Spirit, not that of the group. There may be exceptions, but I believe the old rule is a good one—the circle of confession should be as wide as the circle of commission. If I have sinned privately, I confess to God; against an individual, to that person; publicly, then to the group. There will be occasions, though, when it is a great blessing to put down my mask and pour out my failure to an understanding heart. And there is powerful help in the group, especially when I can testify to the cleansing and victory God has given me in the specific problem.

4. I may discover that my rut is largely the result of fatigue, or monotony. Elijah went into a deep depression after his great victory at Mt. Carmel. In the nervous and physical exhaustion that followed, he fled from one woman and hid in a cave. Someone has said that no man can be a philosopher when he has a toothache, and while a saint may sometimes get tired, it's very difficult to be tired and to feel saintly! Just because we are marching in the

Lord's army is no reason for our feet to be less tired or the blisters less real! We should also beware of monotony. Not all repetition is bad, but even a "good" rut can end up as the vain repetition our Lord warned against.

D. L. Moody used to say, "I am a leaky vessel, and I need to keep under the tap." So may the Holy Spirit revitalize us until our witness has again power and pungency, and men take knowledge of us, "that we have been with Jesus."

Paul's urgency came also in the realm of obedience—the Christ-mastered will. He looked forward to Christ at the judgment seat, backward to Christ on the cross, inward to Christ in his heart. Now he looks upward and sees his Lord reigning on a throne, as he cries, "Now then, we are ambassadors for Christ, as though God did beseech you by us. We pray you in Christ's stead, be ye reconciled to God."

Our urgency is that of the Christian ambassador, under strict orders from his sovereign King. One of my Presbyterian seminary professors used to say, "Young man, do you believe in the sovereignty of God? Then obey your sovereign God when He tells you to go into all the world and preach the Gospel!" En route to the African Crusades in 1960, our plane touched down briefly at Dakar, West Africa. A French pastor, missionary of the Reformed Church, came out to meet us for coffee. We found he had labored in that Muslim center for ten years. One of the group asked, "How many converts have you had?" "Oh," he thought, "one, two—perhaps three." "Three converts in ten years! Why do you stay?" "Why do I stay?" His face mirrored his surprise at the thoughtless question. "I stay because Jesus Christ put me here!"

Jesus Christ put us here; that is our urgency. This is implicit in the very titles that Paul uses to describe the ministers of the Gospel. We are stewards of Christ. "Let a man so account of us as . . . stewards of the mysteries of God. Moreover, it is required in stewards that a man be found faithful" (1 Corinthians 4:1,2). The steward is a trustee. So this word underlines the accountability of our office. We are heralds of Christ. In 2 Timothy 1:10-11 Paul writes of the Gospel "whereunto I am appointed a preacher [herald]." The preacher or herald is appointed to deliver a specific message by his Royal Master. So this term highlights the authenticity of our message. We are also ambassadors for Christ (2 Corinthians 5:20). An ambassador is the authorized representative of his government. So this title emphasizes the authority of our mission.

It has pleased God to join together the work and the word of reconciliation. That work which Jesus Christ did for men becomes effective in men as the Spirit of God uses the word proclaimed by his ambassadors. " . . . It pleased God by the foolishness of preaching to save them that believe" (1 Corinthians 1:21). Faith, says Paul, comes "by hearing, and hearing by the Word of God," "How then . . . shall they hear without a preacher?" (Romans 10:17,14).

Paul most certainly did not believe that preaching the Word of the cross was a sort of elective, since men were already saved. Indeed, he was conscious that the very act of evangelistic preaching could be a means of hardening the unbelieving hearer. "For we are unto God a sweet savour of Christ, in them that are saved, and in them that perish: to the one we are the savour of death unto death; and to the other the savour of life unto life. And who is sufficient for these things?" (2 Corinthians 2:15,16). He recognized that "if our gospel be hid, it is hid to them that are lost, in whom the God of this world has blinded the minds of them which believe not, lest the light of the glorious gospel of Christ . . . should shine unto them" (2 Corinthians 4:3,4).

The so-called "new universalism" and "new evangelism" has failed to grasp the totality of Scripture teachings. Whereas the new universalism says that Christ is both Lord and Savior of all men, Scripture teaches that Christ is indeed the only Lord of the human race (Philippians 2:9-11), but while he is Lord of all, he is not Savior of all. Christ himself taught that many of those who called him Lord, Lord, would be banished from his presence (Matthew 7:21-23). Whereas the "new evangelism" says that all men are already saved in Christ and need only to hear this good news, Scripture teaches that God has reconciled the world to himself in the death of Christ (2 Corinthians 5:19), but men still need individually to be reconciled to God (2 Corinthians 5:20). The urgency with which we respond to Christ's command to go and preach the Gospel will certainly depend on whether we believe that men are not really lost but only ignorant of their salvation, or whether we believe that men are really lost and need to hear the Gospel message in order to be saved.

Paradoxically, it is as we obey Christ's command that urgency and compassion come. We are not just to wait indefinitely until we get a great passion. Rather we should rethink the truths of our commission, re-examine the freshness of our walk with the Lord, and then go out and speak to someone about Christ! How often I have discovered in doing this that, once the barrier of hesitation is crossed and the word of witness begun, the old thrill comes surging back! It is like the athlete who gets out of condition. He dreads to start training again. It takes tremendous will power to begin again that first day as he works out, but once he begins to feel the pull of his muscles and the flow of his energy, you can't stop him!

If the reader will pardon another personal word, I have found that my own spiritual life is usually much healthier when I am in the midst of some evangelistic endeavor. Now that is a confession, I know, of my own spiritual fickleness. But it is also a revelation, I believe, of a spiritual law. As I see people coming to Christ, I relive vicariously my own spiritual birth. It is a renewing catharsis. (This is similar to the truth discovered and insisted upon by Alcoholics Anonymous, that the recovered alcoholic must always give himself in helping someone else who has the same problem, if he is to stay sober himself.) The Christian church and the Christian person remain healthy only as one hand is stretched up to receive from God while the other is stretched out to share with man.

There is a touching story about Brother Bryan, the saintly preacher in Birmingham, Alabama. Brother Bryan was once attending a day-long conference on evangelism in a local church. Late in the morning he became restless and stepped outside for some fresh air. Across the street he spotted a workman sitting on the curb, his lunch pail open. Brother Bryan began a conversation and soon found the man was not a Christian. He lovingly presented the Gospel and had the joy of leading the man to Christ and arranging to bring him into the fellowship of the church. Then he went back across the street and rejoined the crowd for the remainder of the conference on evangelism!

Perhaps when a well-known seminary president said of Billy Graham (with tongue in cheek), "I like him because he never goes to a conference on evangelism!" he was feeling that, unlike Brother Bryan, evangelism in general suffers from too much conferring and too little practice.

This then is the source of our urgency—not merely a cold, theological deduction; not frothy, unstable experience; not grim, stoic obedience; but the ready response of our entire personality to the grace of the Lord Jesus Christ. For he is the Great Evangelist. And it is Christ in my mind, Christ in my heart, and Christ in my will who makes me an evangelist.

Lay the urgency that comes from Christ's saving authority alongside the deadening influences mentioned earlier. Put against a creeping universalism this: "There is none other name under heaven given among men, whereby we must be saved" (Acts 4:12); and this: "He that believeth on him is not condemned, but he that believeth not is condemned already . . . " (John 3:18).

Put against a mechanical ecclesiasticism this: "For in Christ Jesus neither circumcision availeth anything, nor uncircumcision, but a new creature" (Galatians 6:15).

Put against a distorted Calvinism this: "God . . . hath committed unto us the word of reconciliation" (2 Corinthians 5:19).

Put against a man-centered activism this: " . . . no man knoweth the Son, but the Father; neither knoweth any man the Father, save the Son, and he to whomsoever the Son will reveal him" (Matthew 11:27).

And put against an eccentric evangelicalism this: " . . . Lovest thou me? . . . Feed my sheep" (John 21:17).

We are compelled to witness, not because we have acquired all truth, but because Jesus Christ, who is the truth, has won us by his grace and sends us to win men for him.

Samuel Zwemer once addressed a student convention on the needs of the Islamic world, and closed his appeal by walking over to a great map of the Muslim lands. Spreading his arms over it, he said, "Thou, O Christ, art all I need; and thou, O Christ, art all they need."

He is our urgency.

[1]C. J. Abbey and John H. Overton, *The English Church in the 18th Century* (London: Longman's, Green, 1886), p. 313.

[2]Huston Smith, "The Scientist and His Duty," *Saturday Review* (Apr. 2, 1955).

[3]Emil Brunner, *The Great Invitation*, tr. by Harold Knight (Philadelphia: The Westminster Press, 1955), p. 108.

[4]P.T. Forsyth, *Missions in State and Church*, pp. 18-19.

[5]From a sermon by Dr. H. H. Thompson.

[6]Samuel Shoemaker, *How to Become a Christian* (New York: Harper & Row, 1953), p. 74.

[7]A.W. Tozer, "How to Keep from Going Stale," *Life of Faith* (London, May 4, 1961), p. 363.

CHAPTER 3

Total Evangelism:
A Strategy for Our Day

A GREAT debate is swirling about the question of the church's evangelistic strategy. In terms of world missions, the issue was recently clarified through a series of articles in a national student publication. Various leaders earnestly evaluated the history of missionary endeavor, analyzed the contemporary scene, and proposed a philosophy for the days ahead. One assigned high priority to city and student work, gave low priority to "tribal efforts." Another pushed for concentration on tribes yet unreached as the most consistent response to the Great Commission. A third held to the need of reaching first the emerging middle classes as the traditional "conveyors of information." For several months the debate continued, as the editors were deluged with more articles and endless letters submitting yet another and another scheme, or proposing combinations of them all.

The point is clear: public reaction conclusively demonstrated the hunger for a clear enunciation of Christian priorities in the new age of revolution. Paul's advice to the Ephesians is certainly apropos. "Be most careful then how you conduct yourselves: like sensible men, not like simpletons. Use the present opportunity to the full, for these are evil days. So do not be fools, but try to understand what the will of the Lord is" (Ephesians 5:15-17, NEB). As Christians we are to watch where we are going, to "walk circumspectly" as the Authorized Version has it. Don't just wander through life haphazardly without a goal, says Paul, but make each step count. Let God's Word be a light to your path and a lamp for your feet. See that each particular movement you make is taking you toward God's goal. We are to walk not as simpletons and fools, but as wise and sensible men.

The unexamined life, the uncritical way, is deceitful and unworthy of the Christian. A Christian must not act simply because it's always been done, or it's never been tried; nor because it's my idea, or everybody's doing it; but only because he is satisfied that God wills it. We must "use the present opportunity to the full," "make the best use of our time" (Phillips), "redeem the time" (AV). As Christ redeems us from a life of vanity to a life of useful service, so we are to redeem our time. The discipline of time becomes today a primary Christian duty: the assignment of priorities . . . the planning of a schedule . . . obedience—within the flexibility of the Holy Spirit. The urgency of the task comes because "these are evil days." By virtue of our environment, the drifting life will be pulled along by the tide of evil. So we are to "try to understand what the will of the Lord is" —to bring our mind into alignment with God's revealed will. We are not to shoot wildly and blindly from the hip, but to sight carefully until the direction of our life is aimed for the target of God's will.

Paul seems to be saying that we redeem the time not by giving way to a wild, frenzied, helter-skelter rush, but by a careful, planned, and wise walk. We are not to "give way to drunkenness" but to "let the Holy Spirit fill us" (Ephesians 5:18). Control by wine equals passionate foolishness; control by the Holy Spirit equals passionate wisdom. The Spirit-filled life is eager, but not silly. Spiritual wisdom has meekness at its heart, a meekness that makes a man recognize his own weakness and one-sidedness, and creates a willingness to subject himself to the criticism of the Word, of the Spirit and the church.

It is with such Spirit-led humility that we must seek for God's wisdom in our evangelistic task today. What is our strategy to be? As we seek the answer, we must keep two things clearly in mind.

First, we are not seeking to invent a plan, but to discover God's strategy! We are neither politicians nor generals. Our task is not the "making of a President" nor the winning of a war. While we may find help from these secular schemes in relating our message to the contemporary world, our main concern is to understand what the will of the Lord is. Jesus Christ is the Great Evangelist, the Master Strategist. Paul did not "venture to speak of anything except what Christ has wrought through [him] to win obedience from the Gentiles, by word and deed" (Romans 15:18). A human witness is the hand by which God touches, the mouth through which Christ speaks, the tool to carry out his plans. The Holy Spirit gives the divine strategy to the waiting, obedient fellowship. "At Antioch . . . while they were worshiping the Lord and fasting, the Holy Spirit said, 'Set apart for me Barnabas and Saul for the work to which I have called them.' . . . So, being sent out by the Holy Spirit, they went . . . " (Acts 13:1-4).

God's strategy may seem foolish to men, for his ways are higher than ours. Would any strategist have planned the massacre of five young men by Auca Indians in a South American jungle? What a waste it seemed! But in God's strategy, " . . . unless a grain of wheat falls into the earth and dies, it remains alone; but if it dies, it bears much fruit" (John 12:24). So the martyrdom of Jim Elliot and his companions ended finally in the conversion of their murderers. And this in turn has penetrated into highly influential circles of Ecuador, as men have seen the transforming power of Christ. The Christian strategist must indeed possess a keen mind; but that mind must be under the control of God, through a humble spirit and a flaming heart.

Second, we must not confuse strategy with tactics. Strategy includes methods, but much more. Strategy involves vision—a clear-cut sense of what we are sent to do and the best principles of achieving our objectives. Methods can become tyrants unless they are made the servants of strategy. This is why evangelism is always in peril of being stifled by the idolatry of one particular method. We will return to this later.

The strategy to which we are called today is one of total evangelism. This includes three things: goals, agents, and methods.

Our goal is nothing less than the penetration of the whole world. Jesus expressed this both implicitly and explicitly. "And this gospel of the kingdom will be preached throughout the whole world, as a testimony to all nations . . . " (Matthew 24:14), and "All authority in heaven and on earth has been given to me. Go therefore and make disciples of all nations" (Matthew 28:18b,19a). Luke records Jesus' final marching orders both at the end of his Gospel and the beginning of the Acts, " . . . that repentance and forgiveness of sins should be preached in his name to all nations, beginning from Jerusalem. You are witnesses of these things" (Luke 24: 47,48), and " . . . You shall be my witnesses in Jerusalem and in all Judea and Samaria and to the end of the earth" (Acts 1:8). And John in the Revelation forsees a day when " . . . a great multitude which no man could number, from every nation, from all tribes and peoples and tongues, stand before the throne and before the Lamb . . . " (Revelation 7:9).

There is a true and scriptural universalism which beats at the heart of the Gospel. Ezekiel wrote that God has no pleasure in the death of the wicked (Ezekiel 18:23), and Peter said that God is not willing that any should perish but that all should come to repentance (2 Peter 3:9). But world evangelism means universalism in terms not of result, but of opportunity. We are not promised that the whole world will believe. The evangelization of the world does not mean that all men will respond, but that all men will be given opportunity to respond as they are confronted with Christ.

Elton Trueblood has suggested that most of the figures Jesus used of the Gospel—salt, light, keys, bread, water, leaven, fire—have one common element: penetration. "The purpose of the salt is to penetrate the meat and thus preserve it; the function of light is to penetrate the darkness; the only use of the keys is to penetrate the lock; bread is worthless until it penetrates the body; water penetrates the hard crust of earth; leaven penetrates the dough to make it rise; fire continues only as it reaches new fuel, and the best way to extinguish it is to contain it."[1]

What is quite clear is that the Christian is only true to his calling when he is penetrating the world about him. "The Church," said Archbishop Temple, "is the only organization on earth which does not exist for the sake of its members." But what are we to penetrate? What frontiers did Jesus mean when he said, "Go into all the world"? Do you not agree that this means not only the world of the geographer, but also the worlds of the sociologist? Not only the frontiers of Tibet, Brazil, and the Congo, but the frontiers of all the little worlds in which we spend our lives? Surely our Lord would have us penetrate the world of government, of school, of work, of the home. And does he not will us to penetrate those areas of modern life which all too often are lost provinces to the church—the worlds of entertainment, of the intellectual, of the laboring man, of the disenfranchised—the "pockets of poverty"?

One minister was overheard to say, "Some men are narrow. All they can see is their own church. But I have the broad view. I keep in mind the whole denomination"! May God put on our hearts, in all its height and depth, its width and length, the whole wide world for which Christ died.

"The seed is the word" and "the field is the world." We cannot make the seed grow. But we are called to see that the seed is scattered over the whole field. And the goal is penetration. "Evangelism is not a sporadic encounter, but a continuous engagement with the world at every level," said Tom Allan.

If our goal is the penetration of the whole world; then for the agents to carry out this task we must aim at nothing less than the mobilization of the whole church.

We have not been promised by our Lord that the world will be converted. So success is not our standard. But by any standard the growth of the church over the last hundred years has been agonizingly slow. While Christians made up a little less than 30 percent of the world's population in 1868, one hundred years later it is a little less than 32 per cent. Unless missionary work increases beyond present expectations, the rate of population growth suggests that there will be still fewer Christians in the world by A. D. 2000. With the world population growing about 65 million a year, there would have to be about 57,000 won to Christ every day—about 2,400 every hour, about 40 every minute—just to keep pace with the increase.

These startling figures only serve to reinforce a premise that has long received lip service: world evangelism cannot be carried out by professionals. Indeed, Harnack claimed that "when the church won its greatest victories in the early days in the Roman Empire, it did so not by teachers or preachers or apostles, but by informal missionaries."

A church which bottlenecks its outreach by depending on its specialists—its pastors or evangelists—to do its witnessing, is living in violation of both the intention of its Head and the consistent pattern of the early Christians. When Jesus said to his twelve apostles, that microcosm of his people: "Follow me and I will make you fishers of men," or "As my Father sent me, so send I you," or "You shall be witnesses unto me," did he intend to restrict evangelism to a few specialists? Or did he intend that all his disciples should become apostles; that is, "sent ones"? The seed which Jesus planted in the gospels blooms in the Acts and gives us the answer. "Specialists" there were aplenty: Peter and Paul, Philip and Apollos. But evangelism was the task of the whole church, not just the "name characters." Take for example this incident. " . . . There was a great persecution against the church which was at Jerusalem: and they were all scattered abroad to all the regions of Judea and Samaria, except the apostles: . . . therefore, they that were scattered abroad went everywhere preaching the Word" (Acts 8:1,4). Note that phrase carefully—"except the apostles." All were scattered abroad "except the apostles." Those who were scattered preached. Therefore, in this case, the only ones who didn't preach were the apostles—the "professionals"! Persecution exploded into the church. And the believers were scattered like glowing embers from a fire, igniting new fires wherever they landed! And all this without the leadership of one ordained apostle!

The Latin America Mission made a study of the fastest-growing movements in their field and found them to be three: the Communists, the Jehovah's Witnesses, and the Pentecostal churches. Then they analyzed these movements to find their common denominator. Was it their message? Obviously not. Here were an anti-Christian ideology, an heretical cult, and a Christian group. Finally they came up with this proposition: "The growth of any movement is in direct proportion to its ability to mobilize its entire membership for continuous evangelistic action." Based on this thesis, a program of "evangelism in depth" has been moving from country to country in Latin America, training, uniting, and mobilizing ordinary Christians as never before, and making unprecedented impact in the life of these nations.

To be true to our heritage and equal to our present task, our strategy must insist that evangelism be considered the responsibility of the whole church. To be sure, evangelism is not the sole task of the church. The church is called to glorify God, both as Christ's Bride, and as his Body. As his Bride, we worship, offering to God spiritual sacrifices acceptable through Jesus Christ (1 Peter 2:5). As his Body, we witness, demonstrating the wonderful deeds of him who called us out of darkness into light (1 Peter 2:9). The two belong together, for worship that does not lead to witness is spurious, while witness that does not lead to worship is abortive. But we must hold before all Christians their duty both to worship and to witness.

The mobilization of the church will call for a drastic revolution in the relation of the clergy and the laity. For too long the accepted pattern was: the layman pays the minister to evangelize and to do the whole work of the ministry. Then the growth of lay organization in the churches led to another pattern: the layman helps the clergy to evangelize and minister. This was a welcome advance, but still fell short of the New Testament ideal, for it placed the main responsibility for evangelism on the professional ministry.

Amazingly, a tiny mistranslation in our Bibles may have contributed to our misunderstanding. We have been operating on "the fallacy of the misplaced comma" in the fourth chapter of Ephesians! In this famous passage Paul is describing the various gifts and offices which the risen Christ has given to the church. Most of the older versions and some newer ones translate Ephesians 4:11 and 12 in this sense: "And his gifts were that some should be apostles, some prophets, some evangelists, some pastors and teachers, for the equipment of the saints, for the work of the ministry, for building up the body of Christ." The apparent meaning of this is that the evangelist (or pastor) has a threefold task: (1) to equip the saints; (2) to do the work of ministry; (3) to build up the Body of Christ. Actually,.there should be no comma between these first two phrases. Even a different preposition is used. In "for the equipment of the saints" it is *pros*, while in "for the work of the ministry" it is *eis*—or, as it would be better to say, "unto the work of ministry." A more accurate translation, then, runs: "And these were his gifts: some to be apostles, some prophets, some evangelists, some pastors and teachers, *to equip God's people for work in his service . . .* " (NEB, italics mine). Or as Phillips correctly paraphrases, "His gifts were made that Christians might be properly equipped for their service."

The error is a small one in grammar, but a great one in practical consequences. For it now appears that the clergy's main task is not to do the work of the church, but to equip God's people to do this work. The clergyman still has a particular ministry—evangelizing or shepherding or teaching. But this is a means to fulfill his main business: preparing Christians to serve.

In terms of evangelism, the old pattern will not do. It is not enough for the layman to pay the preacher to win souls, or even help him to do so. The pattern is that the minister helps the layman to evangelize!

The minister is like the foreman in a machine shop, or the coach of a team. He does not do all the work, nor does he make all the plays. (Though he is a working foreman and a playing coach!) If a man can't operate a lathe, the foreman rolls up his sleeves and shows him how. If a player can't carry out an assignment, the coach demonstrates how to make the play. So the pastor-foreman or the teacher-coach doesn't try to do all the witnessing. He conceives his main task as that of training the Christian mechanic how to witness in the garage; as showing the Christian student how to have a relevant testimony in the classroom; as inspiring the Christian housewife to be a godly influence in her neighborhood. As a coach, he learns the talents of each player and fits him in the best spot, so that the whole church becomes an effective witnessing team.

Our whole vocabulary of church activity will change, if we really begin to take seriously this New Testament pattern. As Richard Halverson has said, when we ask, "How many ministers does your church have?" the traditional answer is "one" or "two" or "five," depending on how large the paid staff is. But the true answer is "two hundred" or "two thousand," depending on how large the membership is! Every believer is a minister! When we ask, "Where is your church?" the traditional reply is "on the corner of Broad and Main." But the correct reply is, "What time is it?" If it's 11:00 A.M. Sunday, then my church is "on the corner of Broad and Main." (That's where the headquarters building is!) But if it's 11:00 A.M. Tuesday, then my church is in Room 511 in the Professional Building, where Bill White, Christian Attorney, is practicing law. It's at 3009 Melody Lane, where Jane White, Christian housewife, is making a home. It's at Central High, where Jimmy White, Christian student, is studying to the glory of God. There is the church in action!

To use Elton Trueblood's analogy, Christians are not like members of an orchestra society, who hire musicians and a conductor and sit back to enjoy the performance. They are members of the orchestra. Each has a part to play, and the minister is the conductor who helps each to fit in, as the whole orchestra presents a glorious symphony of praise to Christ.

[1]Elton Trueblood, *The Company of the Committed* (New York: Harper & Row, 1961), p. 68.

CHAPTER 4

The Overwhelming Minority

HONESTY forces one to confess that the picture drawn in the last chapter is too idealistic. Theoretically, evangelism is the responsibility of the whole church. But responsibility and dependability are different matters. We must face the actual situation: faithful and able witnesses will be a minority, the core of the committed. For practical evangelism we will have to depend on "the church within the church," the "community of Christians," to use T. S. Eliot's phrase, as distinguished from the "Christian community."

Tom Allan once told how he faced an impasse with the congregation he was serving in Scotland. At every turn, his efforts to awaken in the people an evangelistic vision seemed to be frustrated. Only a relatively tiny group responded. Then one day, at the depth of his discouragement, he was riding the subway. His eye was caught by an advertising sign for a fashion magazine: VOGUE IS READ BY THE OVERWHELMING MINORITY. The phrase lit a fire in his imagination. "The overwhelming minority!" Has God's work not always moved forward by the growing edge, the cutting edge, of overwhelming minorities—Gideon's band, Jesus' twelve disciples?

We often call for (and too little, I fear, pray for) "revival in our times." But what kind of revival? What do we look for? Would we recognize revival if God sent it? I sometimes think we misconceive the revival we need, thinking in images of a former day. We have read stories of frontier revivals where whole cities would be struck down in conviction of sin, by the clear sense of God's presence. Now I do not deny that such mass experiences may come again. I myself have once or twice seen such manifestations. How vividly I recall a deep moving of God in 1950, during my student days at Wheaton College. For nearly thirty-six hours we sat in chapel, brought by the Holy Spirit to a place of breaking, confessing, cleansing, and renewing. The most lasting impression of that time is a sense of awe and quietness. The blessings received from those days will keep me grateful all my life. However, most awakenings of this sort, in our day and in earlier days, have occurred in a community with a common core of Christian conviction. Our culture today is not so homogeneous. Our great cities are cosmopolitan melting pots, mixing people of many different religions or no religion. It is difficult to feel that we should expect to see revival of the same community-wide sort as witnessed, say, by Charles G. Finney in a backwoods New York lumbering village. If this should prove to be a mere lack of faith on my part, as it may, I shall be the first to rejoice.

However, it does seem to me that revival in our age is more likely to take the form of developing this inner core—the "company of the committed" —in each church and community. What we must seek and pray for are not tight and divisive little ghettos of pietism, but groups of believing, obeying disciples who will grow both within the church, by acting as leaven, and outside the church, by scattering the good seed; who humbly but wholeheartedly accept God's call to be "a colony of heaven."

This figure of the church as the "colony of heaven," which is Moffatt's colorful rendering of Philippians 3:20, is a most vivid metaphor for our day, though we must take care to filter out any overtones of imperialistic colonialism. George Webber has suggested, in his book *God's Colony in Man's World*,[1] that the Christian church as an outpost of heaven resembles a little group of colonials, precariously perched on the shores of a New World. This new colony had to live up to three stringent demands. First, they had to keep their lines of communication and transportation open to the homeland, to receive supplies, instructions, and encouragement. Second, they had to stand together against common enemies—disease, hunger, hostile natives. Third, they had to move outside the colony to subdue the wilderness for their king. This was their sole reason for existence.

The Christian church, God's "colony," likewise lives a three-dimensional role with a "vertical" relationship to God, a "circular" relationship to the brethren within, and a "horizontal" relationship to the world without. The strategy of evangelism demands that the church be renewed in all these relationships.

There must be renewal in our vertical relationship to God. Like the colony in the New World, we are utterly dependent on the communication of supplies from the heavenly homeland. What possible effect can our witness have in the world if our contact with God has been lost?

To use a more modern figure, the church is like a radio set, which reaches up with the antenna of faith, tunes in on the invisible waves of God's grace, and broadcasts its witness to the world. But if the tubes in the set are broken, if its "insides" are out of order, then the radio cannot broadcast. And if the church's inner life is in disrepair, it cannot witness.

Can the church be revived? One gazes at the apathy, the division, the jealousy, the materialism, and feels like an Ezekiel set in the midst of a valley full of bones. Surely many a pastor has echoed Ezekiel's sigh, "Lord, they were very dry." "Can these bones live?" asked the Lord. And Ezekiel answered in effect, "Only God knows." But the Lord God commanded, and the prophet spoke his word, and the bones came together, and the flesh upon the bones. Then the breath of God blew " . . . and they lived, and stood up upon their feet, an exceeding great army" (Ezekiel 37:10).

Is this not how revival will come? With an agonizing awareness of our deadening lack of spiritual power. With an honest confession of our total inability to do anything about it, of the failure of our absurd attempts at artificial respiration—our pathetic techniques and programs, our endless flow of words and resolutions. Then, with the recommissioning from our Lord "prophesy" and the recommitment to the faithful proclamation of his Word— "I prophesied as I was commanded." And then, instead of the awful, dumb silence of spiritual stupor—response! "As I prophesied, there was a noise . . . and a shaking!"

God's visitations come in a time of hungering, a time of breaking up, a time of sowing, a time of resting, and then a time of reaping (Mark 4:26-29). The seasons of sowing and reaping may seem to lengthen. But the harvest is on the way.

Charles Simeon, the great Anglican evangelical, who exercised such a mighty ministry in Cambridge, is a splendid example of how God uses a faithful witness. He began his work at Holy

Trinity amid intense opposition. The congregation was completely
against his appointment to his church, and for a decade refused
to unlock the pew doors, so that Simeon's hearers had to stand
jammed in the aisles. Opponents of the "Sims" inscribed on a
church bell, "Glory to God and damnation to enthusiasm." Hostility
was on every hand at the university. But over the years his Bible
preaching, his exalting of Christ, his missionary passion, his lectures and sermons, his Friday tea sessions of Bible study and discussion with undergraduates, led to the establishing of a strong
evangelical movement in the Church of England. He influenced
hundreds of young men, including Henry Martyn, who went out
through England and the world.

Similarly, Canon Max Warren has described the coming to
East Africa of the great revival which has been under way there
for over thirty years. He points out that the revival began "very
quietly, almost imperceptibly." In its later years there were great
conventions, numbering sometimes more than fifteen thousand people from many different tribes and territories. The beginning was
far different. He traces it to two sources—"first the patient laying
of spiritual foundations over the years, the day in and day out
ministry of the Word of God, through teaching and preaching,
through service and through Sacrament; and second the work of
the Holy Spirit in bringing individuals under deep conviction of
sin, and then through them reproducing this work in ever growing
numbers of men and women."[2]

Warren shares an incident which points up how the coming
of the revival combined two elements: the prosaic and the dramatic.
He was discussing it with two African leaders, and one of them
spoke of being baptized and confirmed but not having a heart
knowledge. When Canon Warren asked them if the first missionaries
had not proclaimed the Gospel to them faithfully, both Africans
were most emphatic that they had no criticism of the way in which
the Gospel had been presented to them. They emphasized that the
missionaries had taught them faithfully, but they said, "God's time
for us had not come. Then He opened our eyes." Warren seizes
on this phrase as "an authentic insight into experience. It bears
witness to the incalculable element in revival. The Spirit chooses
His times. In some real sense there is a dramatic element in His
unveiling. But the unveiling is never out of relation to the prosaic
preparation which has gone before."[3]

So God calls us faithfully to preach his Word, until his Spirit blows again, and the dry bones rattle, and the church stands an exceeding great army once more.

The strategy of evangelism also demands renewal in our circular relationship to fellow Christians. The early colonists had an unmistakable unity, because they were all in the same boat. They faced common dangers. Interestingly, this has some parallel to the modern ecumenical movement. Christian unity appears to be strongest not in the "Christian" lands, where the organization is most extensive, but on the frontiers, where the church knows it is in a missionary situation.

This circular relationship refers to our life together—our oneness in Christ Jesus, the fellowship of the forgiven for whom Jesus Christ is the point of unity (Galatians 3:28, Colossians 3:11). Jesus prayed that we might be one, so that the world would believe (John 17:21).

Earlier we saw how our evangelistic strategy is determined by the leading of the Holy Spirit, as in Acts 13, when the Spirit separated Paul and Barnabas for a special ministry. It is vital to note that this leading was given to the fellowship. Who were the people in this fellowship? "Now in the church at Antioch there were prophets and teachers, Barnabas, Symeon who was called Niger, Lucius of Cyrene, Manaen, a member of the court of Herod the tetrarch, and Saul" (Acts 13:1). Take a look at this crew. Barnabas came from Cyprus; Symeon (probably Simon of Cyrene, Mark 15:21) was an African native called Niger (literally "black"); Lucius of Cyrene was from North Africa and probably also an African; Manaen was likely a Roman; Saul was a Jew from Tarsus. The group was made up of two Jews, two Africans and a Roman! Race was irrelevant. So was class. Manaen was a foster brother of Herod, a member of his court, obviously of high social rank. But he is listed among the others, with no effort to play up this big-name convert. E. Stanley Jones comments, "A new measuring stick has been brought into being: it is not who you are, but Whose."[4]

Where differences of class or race, of secondary doctrines or trivial patterns of behavior divide the fellowship, there, I am convinced, the Holy Spirit will not guide us or use us to the greatest extent in evangelism. Such division in the church denies the very work of reconciliation that Jesus came to accomplish.

Paul made a great statement in Ephesians 2:14 which is crucial to this vexing question of Christian unity. "He is our peace," he cried of Christ. This is the crux of Ephesians, of the Bible, of life itself. "He is our peace." The unique nature of Christian faith is that it centers in a Person. It is not just that "he gives peace" (he does that); or "he shows peace" (he does that); or "he makes peace" (he does that). All these derive from the central truth: "he is our peace"—in how many ways! He is my peace with God—the war of sin has ended. He is my peace with self—the answer to my nagging guilty conscience is in his justification. He is my peace with the world: he teaches that God is in control of all things. And he is my peace with other men, for when we all stand before him, we stand on common ground as sinners before the Savior.

Paul illustrates this in terms of the new relationship which Christ has established between Jew and Gentile. He "has made both one." He has not ended the enmity by settling all questions and removing all distinctions. He has transcended these differences by giving to both parties a new and higher and ultimate sense of loyalty, a new center of gravitation, a new status that makes other distinctions trivial and meaningless. The woman is still woman and the man, man. The illiterate man is still uneducated and the professor learned; the Negro is still dark and the Caucasian light. But now all are Christians—and so "if any man be in Christ"—old categories also are passed away, "all things are become new," and no longer is one judged from the human point of view. No wonder this eventually exploded slavery! No wonder this will overcome the prejudice and snobbery of the world today!

So Jesus has "broken down the middle wall of partition"—not the architectural wall in the Jewish Temple, but the spiritual and psychological barriers which partition and fragment man's world. He breaks down these walls, Paul shows, by putting Jew and Gentile on common ground. Both have the same sins (Ephesians 2:2,3), the same Savior (2:15), the same body (2:16), the same preacher of the same message (2:17), the same access by the same Spirit of the same God (2:18), the same household (2:19), and the same foundation (2:20).

The theme is carried forward in Ephesians 4, which again seems to be a key passage in this whole matter of Christian unity. Paul refers here to two unities. There is, first, a given unity of the Spirit, to be maintained in meekness. "With all lowliness and meekness, with patience, forbearing one another in love," we are to "maintain the unity of the Spirit in the bond of peace" (Ephesians 4:2,3). Here we are moving together from the fact of Christ's atonement, in the bond of the peace which he achieves by his death. The use of the definite article here, "the bond of the peace," denotes a specific peace referred to in the context—as Paul has already said: "Christ is our peace" (2:14).

But second, there is a growing unity of faith, to be acquired by speaking the truth in love (4:13,15). Here we are moving together toward the fullness of Christ's maturity. So we have a given unity of the Spirit to be kept, which is efficient for salvation, and an acquired unity of faith and knowledge to be sought, which is essential for maturity. A tension inevitably exists between these two unities. Our task in the "colony" is to accept each other, imperfect and mistaken sinners, as Christ has received each one (Romans 15:7), and to stimulate each other both in belief and behavior to grow toward the maturity of our Lord.

There is great discussion and heart-searching today about cooperative evangelism, about working together in soul-winning with those of differing belief and practice. What I plead for is not compromise on the great fundamental truths centering in the Person of our Lord and his atoning work. What we need is to distinguish between the primary and the secondary so that, with Wesley, we seek unity in essentials, liberty in nonessentials, and charity in all.

A great lesson comes to us in the story of the "Moravian Pentecost." In 1722, Protestant refugees who had been persecuted in Bohemia and Moravia were invited by Count Nicolai von Zinzendorf to settle on his estates near Berthelsdorf, not far from Dresden. There they founded the village of Herrnhut. Zinzendorf was soon troubled to find that these many small groups could not get along, or even agree how to worship together. At last he called together their leaders, and expressed his deep concern. They agreed to his proposal that for several weeks, in their respective meetings, they should preach and meditate only on the cross. At the end of that time they would join in a united Communion service. On the day of the Communion, when the service was over not a soul stirred. The whole congregation was so deeply moved that they sat together for hours, and from that day on they worshiped and witnessed together as the Moravians, who later influenced John Wesley so strongly. So far as I know this is the only church which has ever had more members on the mission fields than it did at home.

It is out of such a fellowship of the reconciled that a true ministry of reconciliation will take place.

Renewal must also come in the church's horizontal relation to "those without." A colony's sole reason for existence was its work in the world. At night the colonists would draw behind a stockade for rest and safety, but by day the colony moved outside the walls, to subdue the wilderness for the king.

Just so, the Church of Jesus Christ exists in the world as his Body, to carry on the work which he began. "As my Father has sent me," he asserted, "so send I you." The church's mission is not only to be built up itself in the faith, and certainly not at all self-aggrandizement. Jesus came to give his life for the lost sheep. And we are called to pour out our lives for the sake of those outside Christ.

It is far too easy for the church to become a sort of religious clique where Christians retreat from the world. Several years ago, police found a Chinese student who had been hiding in the attic of the First Methodist Church of Ann Arbor, Michigan, for four years! His hair was shoulder length, his skin the color of a dead man's. He had been failing his courses at the university and was afraid to face the consequences. So he fled from the world to a church's attic. The parable is too painful to need elaboration.

How are we to get the colony moving outside the walls, into vital evangelism?

Let a minister start by re-examining his own evangelistic vision and concern. Then let him by prayer and preaching, by personal example and practical instruction, seek to lay this burden upon the hearts of the concerned in his congregation. In recent years, a small library of books has been written on the techniques of evangelism. I shall not attempt to duplicate the how of these excellent volumes. Let me simply suggest three possible levels on which to begin an evangelistic breakthrough.

1. The congregational level. A well-planned evangelistic campaign, emphasizing either preaching or visitation, or combining both, may be the springboard to get Christians moving over the first hurdle of fear or inertia. Participation in a united evangelistic crusade may well create the impetus for continued evangelism, as we shall see later. A Nashville, Tennessee, pastor called together several score of his workers in preparation for the Billy Graham Crusade. On cards he had listed eighty or ninety unchurched families, and he assigned one or two of his workers to be specifically responsible for each of them. "Jack," he would say, "you live near the Ron Jones family. Will you and your family take them as your

personal project, making friends with them, praying for them, and inviting them to attend the Crusade with you?" This wise pastor knew that his congregation would be mobilized only as he gave them specific targets, persons with whom they could build "bridges of friendship" across which they could later approach them with a warm Christian witness. Every congregation should have some such evangelistic effort on a regular basis—whether a series of evangelistic services, Sunday morning "guest services," evening Bible forums, inquirers' classes, or home visitation—where Christians can be challenged to a definite contact with specific persons.

2. The small group level. Years ago Charles Spurgeon prayed, "Give me twelve men, importunate men, lovers of souls, who fear nothing but sin and love nothing but God, and I will shake London from end to end." If the many will not move, we can start with the few. I have often heard Billy Graham say that if he were a pastor, the first thing he would do would be to gather around him a small group of eight or ten praying men and concentrate on building up, training, and sending out these men. Many congregations have found the small group to be the most promising focal point for evangelistic concern. A group of concerned people comes together, perhaps at the minister's suggestion, to seek for a spiritual awakening in their own lives and to study their evangelistic responsibility. They agree to meet on a regular basis, probably once every week or two, and to dedicate themselves to a simple group discipline of daily Bible study, prayer with and for each other, regular giving to God's work, and practical witnessing and service. Some of the best material for such groups has been prepared by Lyman Coleman, of Christian Outreach, who originated the "Growth by Groups" method of small group fellowship. Mr. Coleman has studied thoroughly the potentials and pitfalls of small groups and has made available creative material both for groups whose aim is primarily evangelistic, and for those whose concern is especially the growth of committed Christians.

3. The individual level. Sometimes a pastor may be led to start with one man. A certain minister was greatly concerned to start an evangelistic program of visiting in the area around his church. He preached with great conviction on a Sunday morning about the Christian's responsibility to witness, and asked those who were interested to meet him at the church on Thursday evening. Three people showed up—the minister, his wife and the janitor! Discouraged but not defeated, he went to the home of one of his young

officers.

"George," he said, "I wonder if you would spend a couple of hours visiting with me tonight?" Rather reluctantly, George agreed to go.

That evening they visited several unchurched homes, and the pastor led a family to Christ. George returned home enthusiastic. "Pastor, I've never done this before. This is one of the most exciting evenings I ever spent."

When the minister suggested that they make a date to go out visiting again the next week, George eagerly accepted. For six months they visited together once a week. Then the pastor said, "George, you've learned all I can teach you. You're ready to go out on your own. Now I'm going to ask Bob to start going with me, and I want you to take another man with you. And in another six months the four of us will take four more." With just one man, a continuing program of evangelism developed within that church.

The Navigators movement has taught us a great deal about emphasizing this man-to-man approach. Their principle is based on Paul's advice to Timothy, "What you have heard from me before many witnesses entrust to faithful men who will be able to teach others also" (2 Timothy 2:2). Spiritual reproduction should operate by multiplication as well as by addition.

The mathematical possibilities are evident. If a pastor, operating on the principle of addition, should win 120 people to Christ each year through his own preaching and personal evangelism, the church would have made 1,200 converts in ten years, 2,400 in twenty years. But suppose that same pastor should also train just one man in personal discipleship and witnessing, and suppose that one should win only one more to Christ the first year and help that new man to grow until he, too, became a reproducing witness. And suppose the four won four more the third year. In ten years over a thousand people would have been won to Christ, and in twenty years the total would be an incredible 1,032,576!

This series, of course, is a projection which will break down when it faces human weakness and disobedience, for witnessing moves ahead on the basis of spiritual maturity and not geometrical progression. We shall never mobilize the whole church in this way. But perhaps our imaginations can get a little vision of what could happen once we even begin to tap the potential of unused manpower in the church.

The question is sometimes asked where we begin in seeking

this colony—with revival, with unity, or with evangelism? All three dimensions—vertical, circular, and horizontal—belong together. They cannot really be separated. Revival and evangelism must go hand in hand, for "ye shall receive power after the Holy Spirit has come upon you, and ye shall be witnesses unto me . . . " (Acts 1:8). Receiving and witnessing, these are the alternate heartbeats of Christian life. Without witness and evangelism, revival becomes ingrown, grows stale and sour. But without revival, evangelism becomes mechanical; it degenerates into proselytism.

The question arises, then, which has priority: to revitalize or to evangelize? Must we wait until Christians are healthier before we move out in evangelism? Tom Allan's opinion is pertinent. "Generally, we are told that there is no point in doing the work of evangelism until we are better prepared within our own churches. While this appears to be self-evident truth, it involves in fact a peculiar paradox. The only way to prepare a church for evangelism is by the work of evangelism."[5]

This was the experience of Bishop Azariah in Dornakal, South India. Once a year, three-quarters of the Christians in his diocese would spend a week doing evangelistic work in villages near their homes. When asked about the success of the work, the Bishop answered that he continued it year after year, not because they made many converts, but because the Christians were renewed, driven deeper in their prayer life and their understanding of the faith.

Revival and renewal are certainly imperative for effective evangelism. Yet it is as we move out in obedient evangelism that awakening comes within the church. Similarly, our witness will be spurious apart from a genuine, Spirit-given unity. Yet again, as we move out together in evangelism, the Holy Spirit creates this unity. The point is not to decide which has precedence. Renewal, unity, and evangelism coincide because all are the gift of our risen Lord. He is the one who revives us. He is the one in whom we find our unity. He is the Evangelist. Obeying his command and trusting in his presence we must seek to mobilize the church as God's redeeming colony in man's broken world.

[1]George Webber, *God's Colony in Man's World* (Nashville: Abingdon Press, 1960), pp. 44-50.

[2]Canon Max Warren, *Revival: An Inquiry* (London: S. C. M. Press, 1954), p. 58.

[3]*Ibid.*, p. 59.

[4]E. Stanley Jones, *Mastery* (Nashville: Abingdon Press, 1955), p. 137.

[5]Tom Allan, *The Face of My Parish* (London: S. C. M. Press, 1954), p. 49.

CHAPTER 5

By All Means Save Some

THE strategy of total evangelism demands the penetration of the whole world, the mobilization of the whole church, and the utilization of every rightful method. I do not intend to spend much time discussing particular methods. What I do wish to underscore at this point is the total, comprehensive use of every legitimate method. I say legitimate deliberately, for we must avoid the evangelistic trap of justifying the means by the end.

When Paul said, " . . . I am made all things to all men, that I might by all means save some" (1 Corinthians 9:22), surely what he was urging upon us is flexibility, not duplicity. Total integrity must be ours whatever method we use. Trickery is an alien intruder in the tactics of the Christian persuader. "We use no hocus-pocus, no clever tricks, no manipulation of thc Word of God"(2 Corinthians 4:2, Phillips).

Evangelism has had too much mud tossed in its face by the heels of unscrupulous or insensitive men. With shame we must acknowledge that many have scorned the offensiveness of the methods we have used rather than the offense of the message we have given. A young druggist in Canada attended one of our Crusades because he was interested in the music. Later God touched his heart and he was attracted to Christ. He became very friendly, and told us that he and his wife had not attended church for years, mainly because of an upsetting experience when she was a child. A traveling evangelist had come to their town and as a girl of twelve she was carefully coached to respond to the appeal as a sort of decoy. When the evangelist gave the altar call, someone gave the girl a shove, and she started forward down the aisle while the preacher intoned, "A little child shall lead them." She sensed that she was being used in a deceitful way, and the emotional scar left behind kept her from approaching God for years.

We must also beware of the "Gospel Blimp" mentality, as portrayed in Joseph Bayly's amusing but painful satire of some Christians who tried unsuccessfully to witness to their neighbors by a giant balloon festooned with Gospel texts. There is a constant temptation to use impersonal techniques and programs as a substitute for the costly involvement of personal friendship and concern.

However, one of our major obstacles has been a certain narrowness of approach which fails to take advantage of every means which God has placed at our disposal. One man says, "I believe in educational evangelism, period." Another says, "I believe in visitation evangelism, period." Another depends solely on his annual "revival."

"There are two great dangers to evangelism," said an astute observer. "One is to change the message; the other is to refuse to change the methods."

By all means let us preserve and improve what is useful of the old techniques, but let us be open to creative and imaginative ventures into new forms of evangelism. The Christian evangelist ought to be like the householder of Jesus' parable, bringing forth things old and new, methods proven by experience and those that clamor to be tried.

Some exciting new approaches are emerging today. The Church of Our Savior in Washington, D.C., sponsors The Potter's House, a coffeehouse serving light snacks and staffed on a volunteer basis by church members, who are available for across-the-table conversation and discussion which often turns to the meaning of faith.

Dr. Richard Halverson of International Christian Leadership has pioneered in "Leadership Weeks." Twenty or thirty committed Christian men visit a city for a week at their own expense, and at the invitation of a core group of concerned men in the target city. With only word-of-mouth publicity, local men bring their friends to breakfast in a hotel dining room each morning for a simple time of fellowship, when several of the visiting men tell in direct, uncluttered words why they are Christians. During the day the team is available for personal conversation with concerned men, to speak at service and business clubs, and in every possible way to act as informal witnesses. Hundreds of men have been led to Christ through this low-pressure approach, and have been helped by the visiting teams to establish cell groups for study and growth.

The Inter-Varsity Christian Fellowship has ventured onto the beaches at Fort Lauderdale and other Florida points during the springtime collegiate migration. Debates, discussions, hootenannies, and informal conversations have led many students for the first time seriously to consider the claims of Christ.

Members of the Fellowship of Christian Athletes have played a unique role in attracting the interest of teenagers. Jerry Kindall of the Minnesota Twins, Eagle Day of the Calgary Stampeders (Canadian Football League), and other athletes recently visited Saskatoon, Saskatchewan, for an "Athletic Clinic" sponsored by local Christian student groups. High school assemblies in all the city schools provided a forum for the athletes, not only to discuss their sports experiences, but to stress the importance of moral and spiritual commitment. Each evening the team held clinics in football, baseball, and basketball for sportsminded boys, and gave a "soft-sell" witness. On the final Saturday night a school gym was the scene of an exhibition basketball contest between the visitors and local high school teams, followed by presentations from student councils to the men and a brief but clear-cut challenge by the athletes for Christian decision. Many students remained to talk afterward. Hundreds of unchurched youth were contacted who never would have been touched by any traditional evangelistic media.

Faith at Work sends groups of vital, committed Christian couples from one community to another for informal weekend missions. They emphasize home meetings, to which people invite their neighbors and friends for an evening of discussion. The visiting team starts things off by talking of practical ways in which Christ has made a difference in their work, or their home, or their personal problems. It is the warm, spontaneous, and human effort that invariably draws out the interest of many who have never thought that believing in God and Christ could make any difference in their daily lives.

Surely the flexibility and imagination of these efforts are in keeping with the New Testament, where witnessing covered a whole spectrum of approaches. In it we find examples of mass evangelism (John the Baptist, Peter, Stephen, Jesus); personal evangelism (thirty-five personal interviews of Jesus alone are recorded in the

Gospels); impromptu evangelism (Jesus at the well, Peter and John at the Gate Beautiful); dialogue evangelism (Paul at Mars' Hill, and Apollos at Ephesus, Acts 18:28); systematic evangelism (the seventy sent out by Jesus two by two, the house-to-house visitation mentioned in Acts 5:42); literary evangelism (John 20:31 and Luke 1:1-4 both clearly state the evangelistic and apologetic intent of the writers of these Gospels).

We cannot expect any one method to work with everyone. But there is certainly some best way of approaching any person. God may use a combination of many different approaches to win any individual. A man may find his interest piqued through the relevant testimony of a layman at a "Leadership Breakfast." His understanding of the claims of Christ may be sharpened through a well-written evangelistic pamphlet. Home visitation teams from a nearby church or an evangelistic crusade may provide the occasion when he is led to definite commitment. We must seek in choosing our methods to be natural, tactful, patient, imaginative, sensitive, relaxed, and trustful.

Whatever method we use most naturally, let's be sure we have some method. George Sweazey rightly says that the claim, "Everything we do is evangelism," usually covers up a witness so vague that it should be translated, "Nothing we do is really evangelism."

Before we criticize what the other man is doing, we ought to remember Moody's classic reply to a critic who disapproved of his methods. "I don't like them too much, myself," he admitted. "What methods do you use?" When the critic said that he used none, Moody tartly retorted, "Well, I think I like the way I do it better than the way you don't!"

Evangelism in the New Testament combined three strands: *koinonia*—the witness of fellowship; *diakonia*—the witness of service; *kerygma*—the witness of proclamation.

How did Jesus evangelize? He did it by loving (Mark 2:16). He was above all a friend, and especially a friend to the needy, and to "sinners." He evangelized by serving (Mark 1:34). When he met a sick man, he healed him; a hungry man he fed. He evangelized by telling (Mark 1:14). He was teacher and preacher par excellence.

How did Jesus' disciples evangelize? They followed in his steps. Their witness was by loving fellowship (Acts 2:44). Their witness was by compassionate service (Acts 3:6). Their witness was by faithful proclamation (Acts 5:42).

The strategy which Jesus gave to his disciples as outlined in Acts 2 and 3 is remarkable. First he said, "Go." But then he said in effect, "Not yet!" He put a temporary veto on his orders. They were to wait until the Holy Spirit came upon them at Pentecost, binding them into a divine camaraderie and equipping them for extraordinary deeds of service. Not until they could show the fellowship of truth and demonstrate the deeds of truth, were they ready to speak the words of truth. What were the occasions for the two evangelistic sermons recorded in the early chapters of Acts? The first was Peter's account to the wondering mob of what had happened to the disciples when the Holy Spirit came upon them. Their fellowship was so open, so honest, so obviously joy-filled and free, that people mistakenly but understandably thought they were drunk! The second sermon was Peter's apologetic account of the healing of the lame man in the name of Jesus. Proclamation took on the character of an explanation of the unique life and service of these early Christians.

In a full and total witness, these three strands must remain together.

We must evangelize by the reality of our fellowship.

"Fellowship evangelism" is particularly meaningful in our contemporary society. Uprooted by two world wars, bewildered by a constantly shifting society, modern families are constantly transferred from city to city, and change homes almost as often as they do cars! One of every five families in the United States moves every year. One man was overheard on a bus to say that they bought a new home each year, as his wife found it less bother to move than to clean house! Old family ties and social securities are gone. People have lost their identity in rootless mobility, in the "anonymous living" of huge apartments, in the isolation of suburbia. The last U.S. census showed that more than half the nation's counties and all but one (Los Angeles) of the fifteen largest cities had lost population. People are flowing from town and downtown to the sprawling suburbs, where too often they find a chilling lack of community. Is it any wonder that alcohol addiction is rising fastest among housewives, trying to drown their loneliness in a bottle?

Then there are the disenfranchised minorities, the perpetually poor, who channel their longing for a community of brothers into all sorts of ersatz, fake communities—the Marxist cell, the accepting gang at the tavern, the bitter fellowship of Black Muslims.

It is recorded of the primitive Christians, "all that believed were together." This note of togetherness is reflected in the constant repetition of the phrase "one another." The foundation of all Christian relationships was that believers were " . . . members one of another" (Romans 12:5, Ephesians 4:25). Like it or not, in Christ they belonged together. Therefore they were to "receive one another . . . " (Romans 15:7) as Christ had received them; to "love one another" (John 13:34,35) as Christ had loved them; to "submit one to another" (Ephesians 5:21), to "edify one another" (Romans 14:19), "bear one another's burdens" (Galatians 6:2), "pray one for another" (James 5:16), "admonish one another" (Romans 15:14), "forgive one another" (Ephesians 4:32), "provoke one another" (Hebrews 10:24), "forbear one another" (Ephesians 4:12), "be kind one to another" (Ephesians 4:32).

What an opportunity we have to reflect this divine brotherhood to a world grown weary of superficial "togetherness"—to offer to men the kind and deep and honest and open fellowship where people are loved "because of" Jesus Christ and "in spite of" their sins, unlovingness, and weakness.

Tragically, we have failed to let people see in us the friendship of Christ. Emil Brunner closes his book, *The Misunderstanding of the Church*, with these words, "It is because the church has neglected in almost all ages to create a true fellowship in Christ that we are confronted by the phenomenon of modern Communism, which has grown like a wasting disease."[1]

Born and bred in a churchy atmosphere, as most Christians are, we have no idea of the fear many unchurched people have of coming into the house of God. The unchurched person often has a built-in expectation of being rebuffed. He thinks we can smell his sin in his clothes. When we add to his reluctance our reputation for negativism and pious self-righteousness, our judgmental outlook, our cocksure feeling that we've got all the answers, we just confirm his suspicions that if he did come to church he'd get the cold shoulder!

I heard Jimmy Karam express this in a testimony some time ago. Jimmy Karam had been a leader in the Little Rock race riots before his conversion. He was the successful owner of a clothing store in that city, a former football coach, the typical secular and unchurched man. He told the moving story of how his daughter had become a Christian, and she and her husband had asked the pastor of their church to call on him in his store. When the minister, a well-known Baptist pastor, came to see him, Jimmy Karam said it was the first time anybody had ever come to talk with him about attending church or giving his heart to Christ. Pain came to my heart as he looked out at us in the congregation and said, wistfully, "You know, all my life I wanted to be like you, I wanted to be with nice, fine, respectable Christian people like you. But no one ever asked me. Everybody knew that I was a sinner, and I didn't think they wanted Jimmy Karam in their churches." And I wondered how many other Jimmy Karams there are, who would like so much to know the grace of God but think nobody wants them.

A similar story was told to me by a missionary whom we met during our African Crusades. His father had been a minister, and he attended a well-known denominational university in Texas. There he got in with a bad crowd and kicked over the traces. One Sunday evening he attended the First Baptist Church in that city. He was deeply moved by the pastor's message and recalled to the faith of his father. That evening he went forward and committed his life to Christ. But, he remembered, the Christian students on campus shied away from him. They were suspicious of him and didn't think a member of the crowd he traveled with could be sincere and real. No one offered him any fellowship or guidance, and it was not long before he slipped back again into the worldly ways he had been pursuing. What if some Christian had lovingly and warmly put his arm around him, as Barnabas did with Saul, and persuaded the Christians to give him the fellowship the young convert needed? It would not have taken several more years for him really to begin growing in Christ.

This "closed corporation" mentality, a sort of Christian isolationism, has been a constant barrier to evangelism. Many Christians have been so afraid of being contaminated by worldliness that they have avoided any social contacts with unconverted persons. As a result, they have no natural bridges for evangelism; what witnessing they do is usually artificial and forced rather than the spontaneous outgrowth of genuine friendship. Take the case of a university mission, sponsored by what was reputed to be one of the strongest student Christian groups in North America at the time. There were large attendances, but after several days few conversions, or even effective contacts with outsiders. The missioner began to probe, and soon found that Christian students just didn't have any non-Christian friends they could bring to the meetings.

There is a demand for Christians to be distinct, but there can also be a false idea of separation. Jesus was "holy, harmless, separate from sinners," but he was also accused of being a friend of publicans and harlots. J. B. Phillips has caught Jesus' attitude in this vivid translation of Jesus' own comments on what his critics were saying: "The Son of Man comes, enjoying life, and you say, 'Look, a drunkard and a glutton, a bosom friend of the tax collector and the outsider!' " Part of Jesus' attractiveness, which drew secular people like a magnet, was his wonderful love of life, his natural, appealing friendliness. Luke shows Jesus going from dinner party to dinner party, teaching the Gospel to the guests. If Jesus came back today and mingled with gamblers, the skid-row crowd and the cocktail set, a lot of shocked Christians would throw up their hands and say he was too worldly!

We have to avoid two extremes: isolation from the world, and imitation of the world. God doesn't want us to be either holier-than-thou or worldlier-than-thou. He wants us to be like Jesus, who came into the world to save the world. And this demands an attitude both of separation from the world in its sin, and identification with the world in its need. Without separation—the difference Christ makes—we have an audience, but nothing to say. Without identification, we have something to say but no audience. When Dr. Theodore F. Adams, past president of the Baptist World Alliance, was ordained, his minister father charged him in these words, "Ted, my son, keep close to God; Ted, my son, keep close to man; Ted, my son, bring God and men together."

Paul embodied this kind of evangelism in action when he was arrested in the Temple of Jerusalem for causing a disturbance. As recorded in Acts 22, the Roman commandant allowed him to make his defense to the crowd. Paul began by stressing his identity with these people. "There was a deep hush as he began to speak to them in Hebrew. 'My brothers and my fathers, listen to what I have to say in my own defense.' As soon as they heard him addressing them in Hebrew the silence became intense. 'I myself am a Jew,' " Paul went on. "I was born in Tarsus in Cilicia, but I was brought up here in this city. I received my training at the feet of Gamaliel, and I was schooled in the strictest observance of our Father's Law. I was as much on fire with zeal for God as you all are today." Then he stressed his difference from them, by telling his story of the encounter with Jesus on the road to Damascus. He gives the summary of the life to which God called him in verses 14 and 15. Ananias said to him, "The God of our fathers has chosen you to know his will, to see the righteous one, to hear words from his own lips, so that you may become his witness before all men of what you have seen and heard" (Phillips). This call of God is also the pivotal point to balance the two elements of Paul's testimony. Identification with the world and separation from the world are necessary for an effective witness to the world, to lead men into fellowship with Christ.

The powerful effect of fellowship in evangelism is seen in an incident described by Paul M. Miller. There was a pastor in Indiana who made it his custom to visit each church member on his birthday, and to ask for a report on how the member's spiritual life had gone during the past year. On the pastor's birthday, the men of the church threw a stag party. One of them brought as his guest a hardened sinner, who had resisted the efforts of a number of the men to win him to Christ.

The evening was an informal time of clean fun, warm fellowship, and good food. Toward the end of the party, things grew serious. The men turned the tables on their minister and said, "Pastor, you're always asking us about our spiritual pilgrimage. Now how about telling us some of your victories and defeats of the past year?" As they gathered around in a hushed circle, the pastor honestly shared some of the rough spots, some of the conflicts of the past year, and how God had sustained him. A few men led in prayer for the pastor, and they then left quietly. But the unconverted friend stayed behind a while and said to the pastor, "I never knew that men could experience a kind of fun and fellowship that I found here. I never before longed so much to be a Christian as I did here tonight."[2]

As John put it, "We really saw and heard what we are now writing to you about. We want you to be with us in this—in this fellowship with the Father, and Jesus Christ his Son. We must write and tell you about it, because the more that fellowship extends, the greater the joy it brings to us who are already in it" (1 John 1:3,4, Phillips).

We must evangelize, not only by the reality of our fellowship, but also by the compassion of our service.

We must constantly remind ourselves of William Temple's great statement that "Christianity is the most materialistic of the world's great religions," or as C. S. Lewis has it, "God loves material things. He made them!" The doctrines of creation and incarnation drive home the truth that God is "down to earth." He made our bodies, he saw that they were good. Christ came "in the flesh." His body was literally raised from the dead.

Those of us who are intensely interested in evangelism must beware lest we unconsciously fall into the ancient heresy of Marcion, who gave the impression that the God of the Old Testament was different from the God of the New Testament. We must not divide God the Creator from God the Redeemer, so that we are preaching a kind of *Time* magazine Christianity, where God is concerned with only one department of life—the "spiritual things." The opposite of spiritual is not material, but sin. God is concerned for the salvation of the whole man. We remember George Macleod's saying that "Jesus Christ was crucified not in a cathedral between two candles, but in a market place, between two thieves."[3]

This means that when we "preach not ourselves but Jesus Christ as Lord" we also present "ourselves your servants for Jesus' sake." We bear in mind that men are not only lost, bad, and sinful; they are also lonely, bewildered, and suffering. We witness to our Lord not only when we tell of his wonderful works, but when we strip ourselves as he did, and take a towel as he did, and wash dirty feet, as he did. And if our service is not a kind of bribe and not done in an attitude of condescending superiority, then the cup of cold water or the washing of dirty feet may open the door of the heart to hear about the cross.

Many people in our world have grown wary of all religion. Only patient loving service can earn us the right to speak to them. Those who work in the teeming slum areas of great cities tell us of the suspicion with which people greet any visitor. The door opens just a crack. The cautious face looks out. The obvious question is, "What are they trying to sell me now?" If the caller mentions the church, the immediate reaction is, "I don't have time to go," or "I don't have anything to give." Perhaps the first step to reach such people is not to ask them to do anything, or to start preaching, but just to sit down and find out how things are going and how one can help, for Jesus' sake.

Some of the missionaries in Brazil have given us a fine example of evangelism for the whole man. A team of specialists visits a village for several days. During the day an agricultural expert spends time with the men, talking about crops, giving advice about fertilizer, and helping them to solve their farm problems. The team includes a nurse, who shares with the women helpful hints about family diet and hygiene. And in the evening an evangelist holds a preaching service to proclaim the Gospel of the grace of God.

In the complexity of modern life, our service will take many different forms. It will include the cup of cold water—acts of personal kindness which we can all perform in our spare and leisure time. But it should also include our vocational service. We must get past the idea that Christian service is something we do in the church or for the church, on evenings or on weekends. I can witness to the reality of God just as much by a Christian style of life in the 9-to-5 workaday world, by the integrity, dedication, and love which I show on the job. And service will also include my Christian responsibility for social and political action. Sir Stafford Cripps, Chancellor of the Exchequer under the Labor Government in Britain, held in his book *Towards a Christian Democracy* that the church should not get into politics; but he held just as strongly that there should be more Christianity in politicians and more Christians in politics.

Some well-meaning person will protest at this point, "Keep religion out of politics. Let's just preach the Gospel." Unfortunately, we have often drawn back from social action as a reaction to some of the social gospelers who kept talking about "bringing in the kingdom" and who made some particular social issue into their gospel. We forget that evangelical-minded Christians have a great tradition of involvement in social questions—the abolition of slavery and the prohibition of alcoholic beverages, to name just two. Charles Finney, the fiery revivalist, was also an ardent abolitionist who peppered his audiences with exhortations to help free the slaves.

When we take a stand as Christians on some great issue, we're not trying to "bring in the kingdom." What we are doing is bearing witness to Christ as the Lord of all life. A seminary student asked me how Billy Graham could declare he wanted to preach the Gospel everywhere, but then refuse to preach to segregated audiences. I believe I was justified in answering, "In refusing to preach to a segregated crowd, Mr. Graham is preaching the Gospel," because the Gospel is about a God who is no respecter of persons, who will judge all men without regard for their race or class, and who will save all men who call upon him, regardless of the color of their skin or their status on society's totem pole.

Perhaps it would help to show how one of the great evangelistic Baptist preachers of a past generation took a stand on a public issue, and in so doing won men to Christ. Len Broughton was the founder and for many years pastor of the famous Baptist Tabernacle in Atlanta, Georgia. In the early 1920's a typhoid fever epidemic broke out in a new area of the city which had not yet received city services. Four people died. The authorities talked about it but did nothing. About the same time, the city council voted $15,000 to pave a road for an influential politician. Dr. Broughton felt he could not keep silent, so he called up the city fathers and asked them to send two of their men to his church the following morning.

That Sunday morning he announced to the congregation that he was going to postpone the sermon he had advertised until the following Sunday. Instead he opened his Bible and went from one end to the other showing how God is interested in people's material well-being, and that he is just as eager for people to have good water to drink as for them to attend prayer meeting. As he bore down, the embarrassed officials from city hall were wishing they could go out and stop paving the road right then!

People crowded down to the front after the service to thank the minister that he had spoken for them and for Christ. The next morning the money was voted to extend the sewer service and the epidemic was stopped. But here is the interesting point. During the next twelve weeks Len Broughton received into his church on profession of faith over seventy-five people, most of whom said that they had become interested in his church and his Savior because he had been interested in getting good water for those people to drink[4].

Then most of all, we evangelize by the faithfulness of our proclamation.

The fellowship and service cannot stand alone. Some people say, "I don't speak. I just let my life speak." But how many of us feel that we are good enough to "let our lives speak"? Evangelism demands both good works and good words. We are to "let our light shine before men that they may see our good works," but then we must let them know the source, so that they may "glorify our Father which is in Heaven."

Samuel Shoemaker summarized it like this: "I cannot, by being good, tell men of Jesus' atoning death and resurrection, nor of my faith in his divinity. The emphasis is too much on me and too little on him. Our lives must be made as consistent as we can make them with our faith; but our faith, if we are Christians, is vastly greater than our lives. That is why the 'word' of witness is so important."

Some missionary organizations have become so preoccupied with educational and medical institutions that they have almost no time to teach the old, old story of Jesus and his love. Like Peter in the Acts, we must use the opportunities afforded by the witness of fellowship and service to let men know that "there is no other name under heaven given among men by which we must be saved" (Acts 4:12). Otherwise we will be "preaching ourselves," not Jesus Christ as Lord. Like Paul, we are not to say, "I am what I am," but, "By the grace of God I am what I am."

As evangelicals, we have a great deal to learn from some more liberal brethren about fellowship and service. But I believe we also have a great deal to share about single-minded proclamation of Christ. R.A. Torrey once wrote a little pamphlet called *Why God Used D.L. Moody.* Some day, I hope, there will be an article about "Why God Used Billy Graham." Among the first reasons will have to be this: an unswerving dedication to the primary call of declaring Christ. Billy Graham has sometimes been accused of narrowness. But much of his secret has been the focusing of all his powers upon one task. A psychologist was asked, "How does a man like Billy Graham keep going with all he has to do?" He answered, "He has a purpose." Indeed he has! He has resisted all sorts of tempting offers to go on to politics or to become an entertainer. He has refused those who would turn him into a professional anti-Communist or a race crusader. Part of the power of his preaching lies in the intensity of purpose, which is the thrust of every sermon from start to finish: so to present Christ that men must decide. Intimate friends have noted his faithfulness in private conversation as well as in public proclamation; how he guides every chat he can to discuss the passion of his heart.

He once spoke with some of us about the ministry he has had with the "great" of this world, from queens and presidents to corporation executives and movie stars. "I believe God has given me an entrée to these circles," he said, "not because I am Billy Graham, but because I am an ambassador of Christ. I believe that if I ever fail to witness for Christ, these doors will close." Then he shared a revealing incident. An appointment had been made for him to meet the ruler of a Near Eastern country. The interview was amiable and pleasant, but when he returned to his hotel room he realized he had not really tried to make an opportunity to talk about Christ. "My conscience whipped me for several hours," he recounted. "And then I got down on my knees and told God that if I could have a return visit with this ruler—a thing which had rarely happened—I would not fail to present the Gospel." The next morning a call came requesting that Dr. Graham return, as the ruler wanted to talk with him some more. He did not miss the second chance!

God grant that a myriad of men of like passion may come forth to say with Paul, "Woe is me, if I preach not the Gospel."

In a certain great missionary conference in the Middle East, several days of planning for strategy had taken place. Finally the missionary pioneer in Persia, Dr. Van Ness, arose. "Brethren," he said, "I am sure this talk of strategy is always very good. But really we have only one strategy: telling people about Jesus!"

So whether by personal word or tract, by radio or television, by mass proclamation or neighborhood visitation, we shall be saying like Peter, "Why look ye so earnestly on us, as though by our own power or holiness we had [created this fellowship and performed this service] . . . The God of Abraham . . . hath glorified his Son Jesus" (Acts 3:13).

[1]Emil Brunner, *The Misunderstanding of the Church* (Philadelphia: The Westminster Press, 1953).

[2]Paul Miller, *Group Dynamics in Evangelism* (Scottdale, Pa.: Herald Press, 1958), p. 176.

[3]George Macleod, *Only One Way Left* (Glasgow: Iona Press, 1958), p. 38.

[4]This story is related by Culbert Rutenber, *The Reconciling Gospel* (Philadelphia: The Judson Press, 1960), pp. 125-126.

CHAPTER 6

The Role of Mass Evangelism

WHEN one of my friends was studying at New College, Edinburgh, a fellow American student said to him, "You know, I just can't stand mass evangelism." My friend replied, "Really? You don't believe in preaching the Gospel to a crowd? If there were fifty thousand people to hear the Gospel, you wouldn't tell them of Jesus Christ?"

"Oh, yes," he said, "I guess I would, but I wouldn't do it as Billy Graham does it."

"Well, how would you do it?"

"I'm not sure. I don't know how I would do it."

So my friend said, "If that many people were there, you're not sure you would preach to them. You don't know what you'd say. All you know is that you don't like mass evangelism. Is that really fair?"

Fair or not, many churchmen have dismissed evangelistic crusades in just about this way.

We should coin a new phrase, for the term "mass evangelism" is misleading. To many it smacks of mass hypnotism or crowd hysteria. But the aim is not really to win people "en masse" to Christ. "Mass evangelism" is a platform for personal evangelism. It differs from the regular preaching of the Word of God in the church only in degree, not in kind.

The preaching of God's Word to large crowds is no novelty. Think of the biblical precedents. Moses and Joshua did it; so did

Ezra and Ezekiel; John and Jesus; Peter and Paul. Through the Christian centuries faithful men have given Christ to the masses. In the last century-and-a-half under the leadership of Charles G. Finney, D. L. Moody, Billy Sunday, and their counterparts, large evangelistic campaigns have developed into a familiar technique. While its birthplace may have been the English-speaking West and specifically the North American frontier, the evangelistic campaign has been used of God in East and West, Christian and non-Christian cultures, developed and emerging nations. The Billy Graham Crusades have spearheaded this approach around the world in our time.

Critics have attacked evangelistic campaigns for a lack of permanent results, but the scholarly works of men like Timothy Smith, J. Edwin Orr, Kenneth Scott Latourette, John Wesley White, and others have amply documented the impact of this kind of evangelism on social reform, world missions, church growth, and Christian unity.

Those who say that mass evangelism has not been involved with, nor concerned about, social problems should read their history again. Admittedly, some evangelists have been unconcerned about the social problems of the day. But a careful reading of history shows that many social movements were directly related to men motivated through evangelistic activity.

Charles Finney took a strong stand with the antislavery movement and set in motion currents which issued in important eventualities. Interdenominational temperance societies in Britain began in 1830 when a Bradford merchant was spurred by Lyman Beecher's sermons. Elizabeth Fry, the pioneer of prison reform, was inspired by Stephen Grollet of Philadelphia. Elihu Burritt felt Christians should seek to outlaw war forever and his efforts on both sides of the Atlantic form an epic. For over a century the Salvation Army has espoused the cause of the "submerged tenth." Dr. Thomas Barnardo, whose homes have set up a chain reaction of caring for derelict children, was converted under the ministry of the California evangelist, John Hambleton. Keir Hardie, who was chiefly responsible for the British Labor Party of 1900, was a convert of D. L. Moody and became an evangelist in the ranks of the Evangelical Union, itself a result of Finney's revivals, before entering the field of politics. To the end, Hardie maintained his Christian profession, expending his efforts selflessly for the alleviation of poverty. In our final chapter we will touch more fully on the relation of contemporary evangelism to social problems.

Some critics claim that evangelistic crusades divide the church rather than unify it. Admittedly, this danger is present in any great spiritual movement. Times of awakening have produced tensions, and sometimes divisions. On balance, however, the history of modern evangelism would suggest the opposite picture: that evangelism has been one of the strongest forces in unifying Christians.

The modern ecumenical movement has roots in American evangelism in Britain. Archbishop Brilioth of Sweden, chairman of the Faith and Order Conference which met at Lund in 1952, referred to this when he said that "the church history of the last century is a strange spectacle. Was it not in the groups of individuals who were brought together by their simple faith, by their common experience of life in Christ, in the society of the friends of Jesus that the unity movement had its origin?" He names these groups as the missionary enterprise, the Evangelical Alliance, the Y.M.C.A. and Y.W.C.A., and the Student Christian Movement.[1] What is remarkable is that these foundation stones upon which the ecumenical movement has been erected were laid as a result of spiritual revival crossing the Atlantic from the new world to the old.

Church historians such as Ernest A. Payne, for example, credit the work and writings of Jonathan Edwards, and especially his *Life of David Brainerd,* as being the decisive influence in the modern missionary movement. The Evangelical Alliance of 1846 was first suggested in a letter from William Payton of New York to Angell James of Birmingham. Payton had been greatly influenced by the Finney revivals. Lyman Beecher, the revivalist, preached in Britain with strong influence on the Evangelical Alliance. The Y.M.C.A. was founded by George Williams, who was tremendously inspired by Finney. Williams' biographer affirms that "without Charles Finney . . . there had been no George Williams."[2] Apart from Williams no one did so much for the Y.M.C.A. in the last century as D. L. Moody. The Student Christian Movement, which contributed more than any other to the ecumenical movement, rose from the Moody-Sankey revivals in Britain.

Moody's influence upon the life of John R. Mott, the architect of the ecumenical movement, was decisive. Mott was won to Christ by the testimony of J. E. K. Studd, a convert of Moody's Cambridge mission. Mott also received his early training under Moody at Northfield. The influential Edinburgh Conference of 1910 was convened by Mott, who had become the world leader of the student movement. Mott affirmed of Moody, "Others may have preached and written more on the subject of Christian unity than he, but no one has ever accomplished so much."[3] Dr. John Wesley White has made a valuable study of this whole historical sequence.[4]

Perhaps one of the most lasting influences of the great evangelistic crusades in our own day may yet prove to be the promotion of genuine Christian unity. All who are concerned for Christian unity should ponder deeply the roots of the ecumenical movement in the soil of great evangelical revivals. The unity we seek must be filled with the spirit of evangelism or it will be an empty form. As Principal Duthie of Edinburgh once remarked, "The church is most ecumenical when it is most evangelical."

Those critics who allege that the results of evangelism are short-lived should study the effect of revivals and evangelism on church growth in America. Dr. Kenneth Scott Latourette has given an excellent brief summary of the place that revivalism played in America in the nineteenth century, when the percentage of the population with formal membership in some religious body grew from 6.9 percent in 1800 to 43.5 percent in 1910. He has also pointed out the important role that mass evangelism played in the efforts of the Protestant church to win the masses in the great cities.[5] Extensive investigations by Dr. Robert O. Ferm among thousands of inquirers at the Billy Graham Crusades in our era have shown that an encouragingly high percentage continue and grow in their commitments.

In the contemporary debate on "mass evangelism" proponents may pinpoint certain results—the stirring of an indifferent community, the power of a united witness to the common Christ, the encouragement of Christians, the undoubted conversions of outsiders and nominal Christians, the numerical strengthening of the churches. Critics may focus on alleged weaknesses—that evangelistic campaigns are based on questionable emotional, financial, and organizational techniques, create an artificial context for decision, lack social involvement, postpone genuine involvement in mission, fail to produce lasting results, stress superficial "appeals" as signs of commitment, present a distorted message, and transfer evangelistic responsibility from the church to a specialist.[6]

Friend and foe alike, however, often fail to see that the evangelistic campaign today is playing a fresh role in evangelistic strategy. Through such movements as "Evangelism-in-Depth" and the Graham Crusades, new dimensions of breadth and depth are appearing. The evangelistic campaign has become a catalyst stimulating many evangelistic reactions.

The contemporary evangelistic campaign is a united witness by many churches. While it focuses in the preaching of a gifted evangelist, it also mobilizes many Christians seeking to penetrate a whole area over an extended period of time, as part of the continuing strategy of evangelism.

The objection is often raised that mass evangelism is defective in its strategy, primarily because many of those who attend the meetings are churchgoing people. This question goes to the heart of the matter. Is mass evangelism today worth the time, the money, the effort expended? What role does it play in the church's total evangelistic strategy?

The effectiveness of evangelistic campaigns in reaching many outside the church has been established. Dr. Robert Ferm found in his study of 14,000 converts of the Graham Crusades on four continents that 46 percent were nonchurched prior to their decisions.[7] Yet another contribution of mass evangelism is often neglected.

The fact that many who attend crusades are churchgoers is not necessarily a sign of weakness. It all depends on the strategic objects assigned to mass evangelism.

Mass evangelism must be evaluated in the context of the principles we mentioned earlier—that our goal is the evangelization of the world, that the whole church must be mobilized, and that the place of the layman is strategic.

A generation ago, Archbishop William Temple stated, "We cannot separate the evangelization of those without from the rekindling of devotion of those within." Evangelism must begin among those within the framework of the church before it can spread to those without, and this is where mass evangelism can be uniquely useful.

In the New Testament you find concentric circles of people with varying degrees of faith and commitment grouped around Jesus. There were the inner three, the twelve, the seventy, the one hundred and twenty, the five hundred, the five thousand. We must visualize every church and community in this way. There is an inner core of concerned disciples; next, a circle of people who are Christians, but with little intensity of dedication; then the "fingers" who attend church irregularly; finally, the vast surrounding world of outsiders.

Picture the evangelistic crusade as a spiritual explosion, a sort of shell which bursts with tremendous force at the point of impact, with the concussion and shrapnel moving out from the center to the circumference. The most powerful effects will be found near the center. A new creative burst of spiritual energy will be found there, while many an "outsider" is touched by a projectile flying from the center. The effect will also be seen among the nominal or fringe group who (to drop the analogy of the explosion) will be drawn toward the center and into a genuinely vital encounter with Jesus Christ.

It is in the "strengthening of the things which remain" that Bishop Stephen Neill finds the primary value of the Billy Graham Crusades. In *The Unfinished Task* he wrote, "To say that Billy Graham's influence is likely to be greatest on the 40 per cent or so of the population which is not yet wholly secularized is in no way to deny its value or importance; rather the contrary, since in these days when the church is threatened from all sides, our wisest strategy would seem to be to strengthen those bridgeheads which remain to us in the direction of the unknown and menacing world of secularism."[8]

From a mass evangelistic effort should come four specific results that prepare the entire church constituency, and particularly the "lay" members, to fulfill their strategic role in world evangelism.

First, such a crusade kindles concern for evangelism. Daily doctrinal preaching of man's sin and of God's salvation impresses hearers with the theological convictions that undergird evangelism. Christians are morally quickened and fashioned into effective divine instruments. Participation in informal prayer groups and in the meetings themselves results in renewed devotion. The very act of engaging in evangelistic activity is the surest way of fanning into flame the smouldering spark of evangelistic ardor.

Another result of a united evangelistic crusade is the conversion of persons already identified in some way with the churches.

An increasing number of churchmen across the theological and denominational spectrum are convinced that "a large number of church people also need to be converted, in the sense of their possessing that personal knowledge of Christ which can be theirs only by the dedication of the whole self, whatever the cost."[9] Dean Homrighausen considers the church the greatest field for evangelism

today. E. Stanley Jones maintains that the foremost need is turning "secondhand Christians into firsthand Christians." Elton
Trueblood calls for "conversion within the church." And Tom Allan
warned that "it is idle to speak of the lay apostolate to men and
women who have no firsthand knowledge of the meaning of true
Christian experience."

New approaches and methods in evangelism are useful and
desirable. But the evidence is that it still pleases God by the
foolishness of preaching to save those that believe (1 Corinthians
1:21). People are converted not by virtue of techniques, but through
the preaching of Christ Jesus in the power of the Holy Spirit. In
a remarkable way the evangelistic crusade has been used to lead
people into conversion.

Illustrations can be multiplied. There is the Anglican layman
converted through hearing the choir sing "How Great Thou Art"
in Billy Graham's Toronto Crusade, and who has since gone into
the Anglican ministry. There is the theologically literate but
spiritually unawakened Presbyterian Sunday School teacher in North
Carolina, who explained, "I was a window-shopping Christian—like
a man who sees an attractive suit in the window but is not willing
to put it on. I was attracted by Christ but did not put him on until
the Crusade in our city." A group of young business executives
in Oklahoma, all of them nominal church members previously,
spiritually came to life during a Crusade in their city. They have
since formed a witnessing team that has been used to win scores
of other men and women to Christ all across the country. None
of these life-changing decisions would show up in church membership statistics, for they were all church members before these experiences! Yet the gain in church vitality through the spiritual resurrection of these people is tremendous.

Mass evangelism yields a third important contribution—the
formation of small cores of spiritually concerned people. It is
generally acknowledged that a serious need in the church struc-
ture is for small, informal groups of believers who study, pray, and
share together like the "house churches" of early Christianity (Acts
2:46, 5:42, Philemon 2). The average complex church today has
little room for such face-to-face and heart-to-heart openness of
fellowship as Paul described: " . . . When ye come together, every
one of you hath a psalm, hath a doctrine, . . . hath a revelation,
hath an interpretation . . . " (1 Corinthians 14:26). The vital need
of Christians for mutual sharing, confession, encouragement, ex-

hortation, and edification is often frustrated in our spectatorlike
programs where participation for most persons is limited to listening
to a sermon or a lecture. Perhaps the time is ripe for coordinating
mass evangelism with the development of small, disciplined groups
or cells that regularly meet to share, study, pray, and witness. In
fact, unless such a union takes place some of the best effects of
mass evangelism may be dissipated.

Although George Whitefield was in some ways a greater
evangelist than Wesley, Wesley's ministry had the more enduring
measurable results. Said Whitefield: "My brother Wesley acted
more wisely than I. The souls that were awakened under his ministry
he joined together in classes, and so preserved the fruit of his labors.
I failed to do this, and as a result my people are a rope of sand."
Wesley's famous "class meetings" across England were spiritual
homes for the babes in Christ born into the Kingdom under his
ministry. The meetings provided the atmosphere of fellowship for
growth. Today we need a similar reformation within the church,
and the appearance of such fellowships in the aftermath of
evangelistic crusades will do much. This would be in line with the
pattern set at Pentecost, where those converted and baptized as
a result of Peter's sermon "continued steadfastly in the apostles'
doctrine and fellowship, and in breaking of bread, and in prayers."
Evangelistic crusades can stimulate such groups if pastors are ready
for them.

Often at the end of a Crusade someone will come up and say,
"Whatever in the world will we do next week? I never dreamed
the time would go so quickly! I wish we could keep going!" A
spiritual pitch has come about in the lives of many, who are ready
(after a few days' rest!) to launch into spiritual ventures beyond
the routine program. The wise pastor will take advantage of this
spiritual tide by gathering together his workers and those who have
made commitments and helping them to get started in a simple
program. Abundant literature is available to suggest a pattern for
such groups. Problems of tension within the congregation may take
place, but an awareness of such dangers will help to forestall them.
There is always danger in any spiritual advance. "Courage," says
Max Warren, "lies in a choice of dangers." Which, we must ask,
is the greater peril after all, that of fanaticism or that of Laodicea?

Finally, mass evangelism gives opportunity for "on-the-job"
training in the work of evangelism. Many Christians definitely desire
to witness but are uncertain about how or where to begin. An

evangelistic campaign provides such persons excellent training and opportunity for firsthand experience in prayer, visitation, and personal counseling.

Preparation for any crusade should include a preliminary series of classes in Christian life and witness, an item firmly established and followed in the Billy Graham Crusades. After attending such a series, a pastor friend who is a leader in evangelism both in his parish and in his denomination said to me, "I am convinced that the greatest opportunity in the Christian Church today lies in the field of counselor training." And a young Methodist layman declared, "These counseling classes have given me a training and an incentive to witness that I have been waiting for all of my Christian life!" A prominent minister asserted that as far as his church was concerned, the finest results of the Crusade in his city were among many of his members who had served as counselors. When the Crusade was over, these persons continued witnessing and winning people to Christ! We learn evangelism best, not by reading about it or hearing about it, but by doing it.

For multitudes of Christians the evangelistic crusade provides not only basic training and experience in personal evangelism, but also the challenge for unabating growth in spiritual life and witness.

The impetus created by a crusade is like water piling up behind a dam. The water power is harnessed by channeling it into a number of turbines to furnish electrical energy. So the spiritual energy built up through mass evangelism may be channeled through renewed churches, through awakened groups, through revived and regenerated persons, to provide spiritual power for continuing mission.

[1] The Ecumenical Review, Oct. 1952.

[2] J. E. H. Williams, *The Life of Sir George Williams* (London: Hodder & Stoughton, 1906), p. 37.

[3] B. Matthews, *John R. Mott: World Citizen* (London: S.C.M. Press, 1934), p. 106.

[4] John Wesley White, Unpublished doctoral dissertation for Oxford University, "The Influence of North American Evangelism in Great Britain between 1830 and 1914 on the Origin and Development of the Ecumenical Movement."

[5] Kenneth Scott Latourette, *A History of Christianity* (New York: Harper & Row, 1953), Chap. 50, passim.

[6] The biography, *Billy Graham*, by John Pollock (New York:

Mcgraw Hill, 1966), deals with many of these objections thoroughly and fairly in the context of the Graham Crusades. See also my own pamphlet, *Evangelism: The Church's Task in a Changing World*, available from the Billy Graham Evangelistic Association.

[7]Pollock, *op. cit.*, p. 259.

[8]Bishop Stephen Neill, *The Unfinished Task* (London: Lutterworth Press), 1957, p. 103.

[9]*Towards the Conversion of England* (London: The Press and Publications Board of the Church Assembly, 1945), p. 37.

CHAPTER 7

Communicating Christ

A FAMOUS London preacher was recently asked to conduct a mission at Cambridge University. "I hear you are going to lecture to the students at Cambridge," remarked a friend. "No," he replied, "I am going to talk to a group of sinners about Jesus Christ." It is salutary comment to keep in mind as we talk about communicating the Gospel today—a subject about which we have often darkened counsel by words without knowledge. The temptation is to talk too much about today and too little about the Gospel. Dean Inge's memorable aphorism applies: "If you marry the spirit of your own generation, you will be a widow in the next."

Communication means that we must keep in mind basically two things: what we say, and to whom we say it (this is not to assume that how we say it is unimportant). In a later chapter we will try to assess the relevance of the present generation to the Gospel. But first we need to think about the Gospel message itself. One excellent way to do this is by examining Peter's historic sermon at Pentecost—its context and its content. Proclamation that becomes communication must keep both in sight.

In the last chapter on strategy, we saw that Peter's sermon was preached from the context of the loving, serving fellowship. Peter did not speak as an isolated individual. He spoke "standing with the eleven" (Acts 2:14), as the spokesman for the fellowship.

That this context of our witness must be heavily underscored in speaking to modern man was recognized by Tom Allan in addressing a conference at Montreux, Switzerland. "A century ago, a man recognized a divine order, though he did not accept its demands. Today, men don't accept a word from beyond, because they don't accept the reality of the beyond from which the word comes. Words only have meaning when we share common ideological presuppositions. Proclamation becomes possible and relevant out of a context in which the Gospel is incarnate on terms which the secular man understands."

Students at Wheaton College have found that their Gospel teamwork on Chicago's skid row has been greatly reinforced by their efforts to really get to know these men. From time to time they load up a bus with the flotsam and jetsam of the street, the human derelicts and "winos," and take the men out to a park in St. Charles, Illinois, for a day-long outing with games, boating, and a picnic lunch. It is easy to see that what the boys say means a lot more to men who have seen what they are. They have become friends, not just "hawkers" on the street corner. The words are the same ones most of these men have heard for years, but now some of them are really listening for the first time.

One of the ironies of the modern church is that, in spite of an increased interest in evangelism, the meaning of the "evangel" has been obscured. During the Tell-Scotland campaign in the mid-fifties, a minister from the north wrote to the organizers at the movement's headquarters in Glasgow. "We have our committees organized, our literature prepared, our schedules set, our promotion under way. We are ready now to take part in 'Tell-Scotland.' But, pray tell me, what are we to tell Scotland?"

At the time of the 1960 Olympics the *Saturday Evening Post* carried a cartoon showing the runner from Marathon, of the classic story, carrying the message of victory, come stumbling and gasping into the palace to fall prostrate before the king. A puzzled blank look is on his face as he mumbles, "I've forgotten the message!"

All that effort and no message! God forbid that the church today, with such mighty opportunities and superb facilities, should confess to the world, "We have forgotten the message!" We can profit greatly by restudying Peter's Pentecostal sermon (Acts 2:14-40), which is in many ways the classic of evangelistic addresses.

Notice first the components of the sermon.

1. He begins with an explanation (Acts 2:14-21). This takes the form of a personal testimony of how Joel's prophecy had been fulfilled as the Holy Spirit came upon them. " . . . Men of Judea

and all who dwell in Jerusalem, let this be known to you, and give ear to my words. For these men are not drunk, as you suppose, since it is only the third hour of the day; but this is what was spoken by the Prophet Joel . . . " Personal testimony can, of course, be sensationalized and overdone. I heard some years ago of a boy evangelist seven years old, who recited sermons that had been taught him and announced one evening that the following night he would tell his "life's story"! Testimony can have too much of the sinner in it, especially if he has had a colorful or shady past, and too little of the Savior and his grace. But most of our sermons are long on argument and short on witnessing. The honest graceful personal testimony can add great power to a message. Some of the most effective moments in Billy Graham's preaching are those when he candidly recounts the story of his own conversion as a lad of seventeen, and the reality of God in his life since then.

2. Peter continues with a proclamation—asserting the facts of Jesus' career—his mighty works, his death, his resurrection (Acts 2:22-24). Notice also that in verses 32 and 33, he speaks of the exaltation and the giving of the Holy Spirit. We must never forget that evangelistic preaching is not just theorizing about God, or demanding of men. It is the telling of a story—the old, old story of Jesus and his love.

3. He makes an accusation. "This Jesus . . . you crucified and killed by the hands of lawless men." Notice that Peter does not shrink from using a direct "you."

4. He proceeds with a disputation (Acts 2:25-35), showing how the facts of the story of Jesus fit in with the prophecies of the Old Testament. Peter's involved reasoning and quoting from the Old Testament may hardly seem pertinent today. But it was immensely important to his contemporaries, conscious as they were of their history, convinced as they were of the Old Testament promises of God. The preacher was grappling with the intellectual questions of his audience, within the framework of their thought patterns. There is most certainly a place for apologetics in our evangelistic presentation—for taking the honest mental reservations men have and dealing with them in the light of God's revelation. The evangelist is not primarily an apologist. But he had better show that he has done some hard thinking about the problem of evil, about faith in the space age, about science and miracles, about Christianity and other religions.[1]

5. He builds to a declaration, " . . . God has made him both

Lord and Christ, this Jesus whom you crucified" (Acts 2:36). This is the great climax of this message. I only wish there had been a videotape to catch the punch Simon Peter put into these words, and the deep impact they had on his audience!

6. He concludes with an invitation to " . . . Repent, and be baptized every one of you in the name of Jesus Christ for the forgiveness of your sins . . . " (Acts 2:38), and an exhortation to " . . . Save yourselves from this crooked generation" (Acts 2:40).

To my mind, four distinctive marks stand out in this magnificent message.

(1) It appealed to the Scriptures as authoritative. (2) It centered in Jesus Christ. (3) It brought conviction and concern to the hearers. (4) It called for immediate and definite response.

First, the appeal to Scriptures. No less than twelve of the twenty-three verses reporting Peter's sermon—more than half—are direct quotations of Scripture. It may be urged, and correctly, that Peter's authority in delivering this sermon had a great deal to do with his experience of the coming of the Holy Spirit. But note how his experience coincides with the record of Jesus at this point. After the Holy Spirit came upon Jesus at his baptism, we find him quoting, obeying, reading, and preaching the Scriptures (cf., Luke 3:21-22; 4:4,8,12; 4:16-27). It is surely more than a curious parallel that, after the Holy Spirit came upon the early Christians at Pentecost, we find them also quoting and preaching the Scriptures!

The typical method of evangelism in the Acts, in dealing with both Jews and "God-fearing" Gentiles, was to preach the Word of God out of the Scriptures. When Philip encountered the Ethiopian eunuch in the desert, reading the Old Testament, he " . . . began at the same Scripture, and preached unto him Jesus" (Acts 8:35). Paul went to Thessalonica, and at the synagogue " . . . for three weeks he argued with them from the Scriptures, explaining and proving that it was necessary for the Christ to suffer and to rise from the dead, and saying, 'This Jesus, whom I proclaim to you, is the Christ' " (Acts 17:2-3). Apollos followed the same pattern at Ephesus. "When he arrived, he greatly helped those who through grace had believed, for he powerfully refuted the Jews in public, showing by the Scriptures that Jesus was the Christ" (Acts 18:27b-28). After Paul arrived in Rome, he called for the Jewish leaders to come to his residence, where he " . . . expounded the matter to them from morning till evening, testifying to the kingdom of God and trying to convince them about Jesus both from the law of Moses and from the prophets" (Acts 28:23).

But what do we do when we face an audience that does not share our faith in and our knowledge of the Scriptures? Paul on Mars' Hill is an example. Beginning with common religious ground and longing, pointing to their altars and idols and quoting from their poets, he went on to declare Jesus and the resurrection (Acts 17:22-31).

In such a situation, we may wish to start as Paul did. But I am persuaded that we cannot evangelize effectively unless we are finally prepared to use both the message and the words of Scripture. We have got to be careful not to assume in our audience too much knowledge of biblical truth and allusions. We must be prepared to explain and expound. But I am still convinced that it is easier to explain the biblical terminology than to coin a new one. It is far harder to communicate in some of the new psychological, theological, and philosophical jargon than with scriptural language! One thinks of the young pastor who had just graduated, full of his seminary language, who told his first rural congregation that they were "living in a state of existential tension" —when all the time they had thought they were living in the state of Kansas!

Billy Graham's preaching has been a remarkable confutation of critics who say that the old language just won't do. In fact, he told a gathering of ministers in London that he had found in addressing university audiences that the so-called old, worn-out terminology was new and fresh, because these people had never heard it!

It is an easily established fact that Billy Graham's simple Christ-centered biblical preaching, his authoritative "the Bible says," from which many of the critics have turned away, has still reached a remarkable cross section of people. This may be seen in a profile of the inquirers at the Billy Graham Crusades, compiled from over ten thousand interviews. It was found that out of every thousand inquirers who have come forward, one was a lawyer, two were university professors, two high school teachers, two doctors, ten men in other professions, ten businessmen, twenty career women, fifty children, one hundred laboring men, two hundred housewives, and six hundred students. (There was also half a policeman!)

Evangelicals have sometimes been guilty of an unscriptural rationalism in trying to prove the Scripture. I believe rather that its authority is recognized by the practical results in men's lives

when it is declared, taught, expounded, and preached. Spurgeon
once said with regard to those who advocated a defense of Scripture, "You don't need to defend a lion when he is attacked. All
you have to do is open the gate and let him out!"

This is no plea for obscurantism. We need to know the scholarly
issues, to have access to the facts about the critical and historical
problems, to be able to discuss intelligently the way in which our
Bible came to be written; to have at our fingertips, for example,
the recent archeological discoveries which have verified so much
biblical history (discoveries of which the average man on the street
knows little or nothing). But this is really "pre-evangelism." In
saving experience, it is the illumination of the Holy Spirit which
will verify the truth of the Word.

A second mark of Peter's sermon is that it centered in Jesus
Christ. Years ago theologians liked to say that, just as every road
in England would eventually lead to London if you followed it far
enough, so every verse of Scripture should lead us to confront
Christ. Peter preached from the Scriptures, and from the Scriptures he preached Christ. The Bible is the cradle in which Christ
is laid. Our primary task as evangelists is not to ask men to believe
something about the Bible, but to ask them to come to Jesus Christ.
Our Lord spoke sadly of those who "study the Scripture diligent-
ly, supposing that in having them you have eternal life; yet, although
their testimony points to me, you refuse to come to me for that
life" (John 5:39-40, NEB).

The heart of evangelism is to offer Jesus Christ to sinners. In
Wesley's oft-repeated words, "I gave them Christ." Wesley gave
them what Peter gave them: "Jesus . . . a man attested to you by
God . . . this Jesus, delivered up . . . crucified and
killed . . . raised up . . . exalted at the right hand of God . . . having received . . . the promise of the Holy Spirit . . . has poured
out this . . . made . . . both Lord and Christ" (Acts 2:22-24,33,
36). This is the ever-recurring theme of the early preachers: Jesus
Christ came, Jesus Christ went around doing good, Jesus Christ
died, Jesus Christ was exalted, Jesus Christ sent the Holy Spirit.

Here was the core of the New Testament Gospel—the saving
authority of the name of Jesus Christ. " . . . Be baptized . . . in
the name of Jesus , . . . " ordered Peter (Acts 2:38). " . . . In
the name of Jesus Christ . . . rise up and walk," they commanded (Acts 3:6). " . . . There is salvation in no one else, for there
is no other name under heaven given among men by which we must

be saved," they asserted (Acts 4:12).

This was what raised the hackles of the opposition. When Peter and John were arrested, the council charged them " . . . not to speak or teach at all in the name of Jesus" (Acts 4:18). The council did not object to their healing and preaching as such. Welfare work and "religion in general" they did not oppose. But keep quiet about Jesus, they ordered. "Don't preach any more in his name." The name—the saving authority—of Jesus Christ was the offense.

But here was the one place where there could be no compromise. For no man can call himself a Christian until he has come to terms with Christ. Our task as evangelists is to make a man confront him until, like Pilate, he asks, "What shall I do with Jesus?"

One sometimes leaves a so-called Christian church disappointed because the name of Jesus Christ has been mentioned, if at all, only in the most cursory way, as a sort of footnote to the message. We must beware of putting anything else—the church, or experience, or faith, or conversion, or obedience, in the unique place reserved for Christ alone. Christianity is Christ, and our preaching is apostolic only when it leads men and women to him.

Not only is Christ central in Peter's sermon, but the cross is all-important. The weight is not on Jesus, our ideal example, whom we are to emulate. The whole stress is that in the saving career of Jesus Christ, and especially in its finale, God has done for us something decisive, something that man could never do for himself. It is this, declares John Stott, "which turns Christianity from pious good advice into glorious good news; which transforms the characteristic mood of Christianity from the imperative, into the indicative; which makes evangelism not an invitation for men to do something, but a declaration of what God has already done in Christ."[2]

Preaching Christ does not mean a challenge to men to do again what Jesus has done before. It means challenging men to repent, be baptized, and follow him precisely because they believe that God in Christ has done something they never could do. There is a vast difference between these two approaches. The distinction between *kerygma* and *didache* is far more than academic. Is the evangelist a sort of moral cheerleader, who stands on the bank of the river watching the swimmer gamely struggling upstream against the current and encouraging him to try harder? Or is the Christian evangelist one who sees the struggling swimmer caught in the whirlpool of sin and about to go down for the third time, and throws

him the rope of the Gospel, or better still, jumps in with the rope
and saves him from inevitable death?

The cross is vital to our preaching, for it is here that Jesus
Christ becomes either the stone of stumbling or the rock of salvation. It is in the cross that man's sinful pride faces its ultimate test.
The atonement is crucial, because it strikes at the very heart of
sin—not what a man does but what he is, his egocentricity, his
demand to run his own life and to be ultimately responsible for
his own decisions. Whatever other responsibilitiy a man may bear
for his life, there is one which he cannot bear—and that is the
responsibility for his sin and guilt against God. That, another must
bear for him.

James Denney once said that the cross is like the barb on the
fisherman's hook. He told of a friend who had lost his bait while
fishing, without catching anything. When he pulled his line in, he
found that the barb had broken off, so that the fish had taken the
bait but escaped. So, said Denney, "The condemnation of our sins
in Christ upon His cross is the barb on the hook. If you leave that
out of your Gospel, I do not deny that your bait will be taken, but
you will not catch men. You will not create in sinful human hearts
that attitude to Christ which created the New Testament. You will
not annihilate pride, and make Christ the Alpha and Omega in man's
redemption."[3]

If it is true, as Sam Shoemaker insisted, that 90 percent of
the people in our churches believe Christianity is a simple religion
of moral ideals and behavior, then our task is to make clear that
though Christianity is concerned with right and wrong, it makes
bad people good as a by-product of making dead people alive toward
God, through the message of Christ crucified.

Not only is the cross vital to this Pentecostal preaching, but
the exaltation is climactic. " . . . know assuredly that God has made
him both Lord and Christ, this Jesus whom you crucified" (Acts
2:36). The resurrection, the ascension, and the shedding forth of
the Holy Spirit were proof that Jesus was in control at the power
center of all reality.

The disciples who prayed in that Upper Room after Jesus had
left were like men huddled in a dark cabin on a stormy night,
without lights, because the storm has caused damage at the
transformer. They are waiting for one of their number, who is
stumbling through the black night, the torrents of rain, and the
crackling lightning to find his way to the powerhouse and repair

the breakdown. For long minutes they wait . . . and suddenly the lights come flashing on. "He's there! He's made it!" someone cries. That was what happened for the disciples. The Holy Spirit had invaded them. The power was on! The world was illuminated! They knew that Jesus had made it!

"Being . . . exalted at the right hand of God," said Peter, "and having received from the Father the promise of the Holy Spirit, he has poured out this." And then he quoted David, "The Lord said to my Lord, Sit at my right hand, till I make thy enemies a stool for thy feet." Jesus was, to put it colloquially, "God's right-hand man." He was in charge! So, notes Prof. F. F. Bruce, "The first apostolic sermon leads up to the apostolic creed: 'Jesus is Lord' (cf. Romans 10:9; 1 Corinthians 12:3; Philippians 2:11)—'Lord' not only as the bearer of a courtesy title, but as bearer of the 'name which is above every name' (Philippians 2:9)."[4]

The preaching of Christ as Lord has great pertinence for our day. It speaks powerfully to the human condition—the emptiness which is so typical of our culture and which we shall examine more fully in the next chapter. The fear of being lost for eternity, or of being sentenced to a fiery hell, was real to most of our grandfathers and perhaps to our fathers. But most people in modern times are not conscious of such a fear, or at least will not admit to having it. They are afraid of old age and insecurity. They are afraid of nuclear warfare or cancer. They do feel that somehow their lives have lost any real direction and meaning. As the novelist Peter De Vries makes one of his characters say, they feel that life is like a great safe; it has a combination, but the combination has been locked inside and there is no way to get at it.

Now, the Bible makes it clear that men are guilty. Men are condemned. Men are eternally lost. But what if men don't realize or admit this truth? Where do we start? I believe that this nerve of meaning is our most sensitive avenue of approach to many people today. People, east and west, are empty and purposeless, and willing to admit their "lostness" in that sense. They feel, "There is no meaning left in life." And at the bottom of this emptiness is the pagan opposition of soul to body, of eternity to time. The Greeks thought of space and time as a circle in which the soul is imprisoned until it escapes into the ideal world. History is a series of cycles, repeated over and over, without beginning or ending. It is like a continuous showing of a movie. At first you think that it has a beginning and an end. But if you sit long enough and see it through several times, you may end up thoroughly confused, with the end coming before the beginning, and the beginning coming after the end. You can come at any point and know that you will see the same thing. When you have seen it once, you have seen it all. There is nothing new.

This makes life essentially meaningless. The chart of man's meanderings is like "a set of tracks made by a drunken fly with feet wet with ink, staggering across a piece of white paper." History is a road that leads nowhere. Philosophy is "a blind man in a dark room searching for a black cat that isn't there."

To this the Christian may answer, Jesus Christ is Lord! History is the story of his program. The exaltation of Jesus Christ to God's right hand is tied in to the end of history. He is there "till his enemies are made his footstool." Notice how Paul quotes this same passage in 1 Corinthians 15: "Then comes the end, when he delivers the kingdom to God the Father . . . for he must reign until he has put all his enemies under his feet" (1 Corinthians 15:24,25). Jesus Christ is reigning now. He is Lord. The proof of this is his presence in the life of the church by the Holy Spirit. And the Holy Spirit is not only the representative of the hidden Christ; he is the spirit of promise, a foretaste of heaven, a "fragment of the future age," the down payment which assures that the full payment will come. Life has meaning because Jesus Christ is in control, and history has direction because Jesus Christ is its end. We are moving toward that great climax where every knee shall bow and every tongue confess that Jesus Christ is Lord. The return of Christ will mean an unveiling *(apokalupsis)*, a manifestation *(epiphaneaeia)*, the presence *(parousia)* to and among all men of the Lordship of Christ, which even now is evident to faith.

Though life to the unbeliever may be like a scroll, rolled up and sealed, its message hidden, the Christian knows that the Lion of the tribe of Judah has broken the seal, and unrolled the scroll (Revelation 5). He does not live in ignorance. He has been told who he is and why he is here.

Every great awakening has had some one great theme. In the evangelical revival it was, for Whitefield, "You must be born again." If I were to venture a guess at today's great theme, it might be this verse: " . . . Christ in you, the hope of glory" (Colossians 1:27). Past victory, present reality, and future hope—all are encompassed here. "Christ"—the victorious Lord himself who demands complete allegiance and commitment to himself and his kingdom.

"Christ in you"—present in the life of the believer by his Holy Spirit, to give to life the dimension and dynamism that make zestful, purposeful living. "Christ in you the hope of glory"—supplying the hope of a real meaning to history, of the sure coming of his kingdom, of his own personal return, and a vision of God's glory which is man's ultimate goal. "He being exalted at the right hand of God, and having received from the Father the promise of the Holy Spirit, has poured out this!"

[1]For a good example of a liberal evangelical facing these questions, see Leonard Griffith, *Barriers to Christian Belief* (London: Hodder & Stoughton, 1962).

[2]John Stott, "The Meat of the Gospel," *Decision*, January, 1962, p.4.

[3]*Studies in Theology* (London: Hodder & Stoughton, 1895), pp. 127-128.

[4]F.F. Bruce, *The Book of the Acts, New International Commentary on the New Testament* (London: Marshall, Morgan and Scott, 1954), p. 73.

CHAPTER 8

The Conviction of Sin

THE third mark we note in Peter's sermon is that it brought conviction and concern to the hearers. "Now when they heard this they were cut to the heart, and said to Peter and the rest of the apostles, ' . . . Brethren, . . . what shall we do?' " (Acts 2:37). It is not recorded that they were "impressed by his learning" or "stimulated by his ideas" or "intrigued by his literary allusions" or "amused by his good humor," but that they were "cut to the heart."

One wonders whether Peter would have received a passing grade from his homiletics professor if he had preached this sermon at a theological seminary today! Our soft-soap evangelism is so anxious not to disturb anyone. Some caustic critic of modern ways of winning church members has said that the older evangelism at least disturbed its prospects and made them ashamed of what they were, but now you can join the church and hardly feel it. Your business associates won't notice it, your wife won't notice it, your relatives won't notice it, strangers won't notice it, even God won't notice it!

A bulletin issued by the Council of Churches in a large city, for the guidance of speakers on its radio programs, typifies this approach: "Subject matters should project love, joy, courage, hope, faith, trust, good-will. Generally avoid criticism, controversy. In a very real sense we are 'selling' religion. Therefore, training of Christians on cross bearing, sacrifice, and service, *calling sinners to repentance*, these are out of place. As apostles can we not extend an invitation in effect: 'Come in and enjoy our privileges, meet good friends, see what God can do for you'?" (Italics mine.)

How much easier and smoother this sounds than the jarring preaching at Pentecost! How much more comfortable and appealing it is! How much less potent would Peter have been if he had tried the modern plan. Would hearts have been changed if they had not been cut?

There is a considerable area of disagreement today over this whole matter of the conviction of sin in evangelistic preaching. On the one hand, there is strong opinion that we have not had enough preaching on sin and repentance. The law must be preached before the Gospel to awaken the conviction of sin, or the unawakened sinner will have only an easy, nominal, and useless faith. John Wesley's famous strategy is esteemed. Wesley said that when he first went to a place he preached "the law in the strongest, the closest, the most searching manner possible." Only as people became convinced of sin did he "mix more and more of the Gospel . . . to raise into spiritual life, those whom the law hath slain." Wesley warned that the Gospel was not to be preached too hastily, because of the danger that many who were convinced would heal their own wounds slightly.

Dr. Martyn Lloyd-Jones of Westminster Chapel, London, holds strongly to this position, as seen in the following passage from his excellent studies on the Sermon on the Mount, "There is no true evangelism without the doctrine of sin . . . the essence of evangelism is to start by preaching the law; and it is because the law has not been preached that we have had so much superficial evangelism . . . This means that we must explain that mankind is confronted by the holiness of God, by His demands, and also by the consequences of sin . . . It is only the man who is brought to see his guilt . . . who flies to Christ for deliverance. True evangelism . . . is primarily a call to repentance."[1]

The late Dr. W. E. Sangster, the esteemed English Methodist, took a similar position in his fine little volume, *Let Me Commend*: "Preaching the Gospel should always be preceded by preaching the moral law . . . the moral law is what God demands, and what our consciences confirm as being due. Only people inwardly distressed by conscious failure are likely to hear the Gospel as good news. To all the rest, it is perilously near to casting pearls to swine."[2]

At the other pole, there is a group which strenuously opposes the traditional order of first law, then Gospel. J. B. Phillips in a number of his popular writings has criticized the evangelist who, according to him, first seeks to induce a sense of guilt by various means, and then to pressure people—whose sensitive consciences have been touched by these emotional pleadings—into what is often a premature decision.

Karl Barth, of course, has been extremely vocal on this whole matter. Whereas men like Phillips would criticize the traditional evangelistic method on the ground of practice, Barth criticizes it on the level of theology. Dr. Barth's concern is to avoid setting up an autonomous "law" which is independent from the Gospel. Referring to Paul's statement in Romans 3:20 that the law discloses sin, he says,

We wrest this statement from its context and misunderstand it if we take it to mean, as some did, that there is a Law, which is different from the Gospel, a Law by which we are confronted and have to be confronted if we are to come to a knowledge of sin and to be led to repentance and to become receptive and ready for the Gospel. The Law of which Paul speaks in Romans 2-3 is the Law of God, which, as the Law of His covenant of grace, calls men away from any attainment of his own righteousness to repentance and obedience in the form of trust in God's goodness. It is the Law which Paul does not interpret apart from the Gospel, but in the Gospel.[3]

"Law" to him is grace under the form of law. Barth recognizes a certain "practical strength" in the approach of the reformers, putting law before Gospel, and says:

By a happy inconsistency they could and can produce serious results. But if we do not want the consequences we must not want the presupposition. We must not allow the example of Reformation theology (which was graciously preserved from the consequences) to mislead us into tempting God . . . the incline obviously begins at the point where we think we have to create the message of sin from some other source than . . the message of Jesus Christ. [So he asks,] Why must the doctrine of sin precede Christology? . . . only when we know Jesus Christ do we really know that man is the man of sin, and what sin is, and what it means for man.[4]

Four reasons are given by Barth to show why conviction of sin can never be separated from Christ. First, it is because sin is seen in its "purest" form in relation to Christ. Where, asks Barth, do we see the "three moments of evil, rebellion against God, enmity with one's neighbor, and sin against one's self"? The answer, says Barth is in Christ, because the Christ whom man offends is God meeting him in the flesh, because the Christ whom man murders is the fellowman in whose image God has made every man, because the Christ whom he suppresses is the eternal Word of God by whom all things are made.[5]

Second, says Barth, Christ is the judge who discloses the sinfulness of sin, because he alone is really man's rightful Lord. He alone, who is both God and man, "has the authority and competence to say that the direction of human being and thought and activity . . . is forbidden and wrong."[6]

Third, says Barth, in Jesus Christ, sin is shown not as an accident, but as the truth of all of man's being and activity. He makes it impossible to think that we are more or less guilty because we have committed "big" or "little" sins. "All sin, great and small, flagrant or less obvious, needed and needs to have been and to be borne by him."[7]

And finally, it is in Christ that we see the significance of sin. Its seriousness is measured by God's only possible reaction, the coming of Jesus Christ himself. "It was not necessary that God should become man and that the Son of God should die on the cross simply to deal with an interruption in the course of the world, simply to mitigate the relative imperfection of the human situation. . . . The serious and terrible nature of human corruption . . . can be measured by the fact that the love of God could react and reply to this event only by His giving . . . of Jesus Christ Himself."[8]

It is enlightening to notice what the experience of some missionaries has been with regard to the conviction of sin. Bishop Linton, one of the most successful evangelists among Muslims ever sent out from the Church of England, was once asked what he found to be the element of Christianity which appealed most to the Muslims in Persia. His answer was that "it was the Person and Character of Christ, not conviction of sin. The sense of sin developed in converts, but it played no part in their conversion."[9]

A. Paget Wilkes, cofounder of the Japan Evangelistic Band, has a most helpful discussion of this subject in his classic on the sacred art of soul-winning, *The Dynamic of Service*. Though it was written a number of years ago, it has been reprinted and it is still fresh and stimulating. Drawing on his wide experience in both

England and Japan, Wilkes made a distinction between the "sense of need" and the "sense of sin."

"In so-called Christian lands . . . it is sin against God that we need to emphasize. In heathen lands, however, the case is obviously far otherwise. Before there can be the sin of rejection, there must be a knowledge of what has been offered; before men can be convicted of sin in the deeper sense of the term, there must be a presentation of the Gospel blessing, and an appeal to their sense of need, rather than of sin; and yet I hasten to add that there can be no true and lasting experience of salvation without conviction of sin." He also "observed that the sense of sinner-hood comes later. The soul moves backward, so to speak; he obtains deliverance . . . and then as he is instructed . . . he learns the magnitude and depth of the mercy of God in pardoning his transgressions."[10]

I have seen an example of what Paget Wilkes refers to here as the soul moving backward, in the life of a very close friend and associate in the ministry, and this took place in "Christian" America! This man after a distinguished career in the Naval Air Force had become an entertainer, singing with big-name bands and in night clubs. In Las Vegas he met a young lady, a dancer, whom he married. After several years his life began to fall apart. He was drinking too heavily; he and his wife were fighting constantly; he had even contemplated suicide. Then one day in a Louisville, Kentucky, motel room he and his wife decided to start reading the Bible. He read through the first three Gospels and was not particularly impressed. The resurrection especially was a stumbling block. But as he came to the conclusion of John's Gospel, and read the story of Thomas, he identified with this doubter. "Here is an honest man," he thought. "He doesn't believe it either!" As he read on, however, through the story of Thomas' encounter with the living Christ, he was deeply moved, and remembers turning to his wife and saying, "I don't understand all about this. But I am sure of one thing now. Jesus Christ is not dead. He is alive some place, and I mean to find him."

Shortly after, he and his wife decided to go to church on Sunday morning, although neither had attended regularly for years. It happened to be Layman's Sunday, and they heard a local businessman talk on the practice of tithing. When they got back to their room, his wife wanted to start tithing, but my friend felt they didn't have enough money to do this. But finally after some time of arguing, and out of spite, to show his wife that they would run out of money, he agreed, and they sent a small amount to their old churches, one that he had attended as a boy in Mississippi and her home church in Illinois. In a very amazing way, an income tax refund check from the government was forwarded to them several days later just when they had run out of cash. Soon after, he left show business and went to work in a hotel and banking concern in Florida. There he learned to find God's guidance in prayer, and eventually was so overwhelmed by the power of the living Christ that he entered the ministry. Now here is the interesting thing. My friend once told me, "I believe I knew Jesus Christ as Lord, before I knew him as Savior. I understood the power of his resurrection, before I ever really grasped why he had died for me on the cross." He came to a very real sense of sin, and of gratitude to God for the atonement, but he did not first come to Christ at that point!

It seems to me that the two views presented here are opposite sides of the same coin. Without a knowledge of sin, we cannot appreciate Jesus Christ; but without a knowledge of Christ, we cannot appreciate the sinfulness of our sin!

Let me conclude this discussion with several observations.

1. Conviction of sin is the work of the Holy Spirit. Jesus said of the Spirit " . . . I will send him to you. And when he comes, he will convince the world of sin and of righteousness and of judgment" (John 16:7b-8). At Pentecost, Peter preached and the Spirit accompanied his preaching with convicting and converting power. Peter and the apostles later said to the council, " . . . we are witnesses to these things, and so is the Holy Spirit whom God has given to those who obey him" (Acts 5:32). We must beware of seeking to induce guilt by some mere psychological technique. Neither clever oratory, nor logical persuasion, nor angry denunciation can bring men to a true sense of sin. "Have we forgot that this is a work for two?" asks Prof. J. B. Green. "Have we been attempting to do our part and that of the Spirit also? Or have we never heard, or having heard have we forgot that there is a Holy Spirit, the coefficient of all true preaching?" It is not within our power to convince and convert the world. That is the office of the Holy Spirit. Only his still small voice can make a man say, "Against thee, thee only, have I sinned."

2. We must remember that conviction is not just of "sins" but of sin and its sinfulness, of our offense against a Holy God and our separation from him. I have noted in evangelistic Crusades that

when I invite those who have come forward as inquirers to repeat a prayer after me, instead of praying, "Forgive my sin," singular, many or most people will pray, "Forgive my sins"—the plural. Men think of sin as what we do, not so much as what we are. But a man needs to know not only that he is bad, but that he is lost; not so much that he has sinned, but that he is a sinner. The deepening of the sense of sin is evident in David's penitential psalm. He begins by asking God to "blot out my transgressions." Then he feels the need to have God cleanse him. He goes on to reveal a constant pressure from his failure, "My sin is ever before me." And then he realizes that his sin is not only a matter of personal weakness, or of social transgression, but that it is a failure in his obligations to the Almighty. "Against thee, thee only, have I sinned, and done this evil in thy sight." His sin is then seen, not as a momentary lapse, but as the tenor and direction to which his whole life has tended from infancy. "Behold, I was shapen in iniquity, and in sin did my mother conceive me." And finally, he is driven to the depths of brokenness as the understanding comes to him that what God desires is not only conformity in the outward act, but purity in the inner attitude. "Behold, thou desirest truth in the inward parts." So is David convicted of sin; so does he learn the meaning of a broken and a contrite heart (Psalm 51:1-6,17).

J. I. Packer succinctly distinguishes between the natural sense of shortcoming and conviction of sin. "Everyone's life includes things which cause dissatisfaction and shame . . . [but] the bad conscience of the natural man is not at all the same as conviction of sin . . . to preach sin means, not to make capital out of people's felt frailties (the brainwashers' trick), but to measure their lives by the Holy Law of God."[11]

3. We must also remember that the particular approach to any individual will vary. There is no pat formula. The ministry of Jesus gives us an important clue. It is revealing that Jesus reserved his scathing denunciation of sin for the moral and religious leaders of the day, those whose outward lives were exemplary, the self-righteous Pharisees (see his "woes" in Matthew 23). But he welcomed flagrant sinners with no word of condemnation (Mark 2:14-15, Luke 7:36-37, John 8:1-11).

Perhaps our approach will depend somewhat on the religious background of the person we are dealing with. If we live in a "post-Christian" era, then our approach to the modern pagan, as with our missionary friends quoted above, may be first along the line of the person of Christ and of man's need—for purpose, for deliverance, for joy, for understanding—then leading to the truth of sin.

I have been impressed in this connection with the approach taken by the Young Life movement, which emphasizes friendship contacts with unchurched high-schoolers, and informal house-meetings. Over the period of a year, these weekly meetings will follow a definite sequence. The leader begins the year for a number of weeks with brief and informal talks about the person of Jesus Christ. After dealing with the claims of Christ, his person, and his influence, he will then move on to deal with man, his need and his sin, and then come to the truths of the cross, of decision, and of discipleship.

My own thinking has somewhat changed at this point. At one time, in giving a series of evangelistic talks or messages, I would begin with a message on the human dilemma, man's predicament, the fact of sin and the like, and then in succeeding messages deal with the person of Christ. But in recent times I have felt that the reverse order is more effective, particularly in speaking to audiences where one knows there are large numbers of nonprofessing Christians.

An interesting conversation with two young men, one a staff member of a student Christian organization and the other a clergyman, highlighted for me the two sides of this issue. We were talking about the conviction of sin, and these men shared their experiences. The student worker had been brought up in a nonChristian home. Not until his final year in high school did he come to make some Christian friends and to be introduced to the claims of Christ through the meetings of their group at his school. As he recalled, there was no particular sense of sin when he became a Christian. He was attracted by the obvious joy and purpose and assurance of these Christians. He longed for that kind of peace and certainty. Not until after he had become a Christian and began to measure his life by the demands of discipleship, did he realize how far short he had fallen. The young clergyman, on the other hand, had been brought up in a Christian home. All his life he had attended church and believed the truths of basic Christianity. In his case there was a long period of struggle, of inner turmoil, of tormenting by his conscience, of wrestling with the knowledge of his sinnerhood, before the burden rolled off, as with Christian in Pilgrim's Progress, and he was free.

4. We must ask, what means does the Holy Spirit use to bring conviction of sin?

First, there is the preaching of the Word of God, which the writer to the Hebrews tells us is " . . . living and active, sharper than any two-edged sword, piercing to the division of soul and spirit, of joints and marrow, and discerning the thoughts and intentions of the heart" (Hebrews 4:12). It is by the declaration of the Word of God, especially of his holy standard, declared in the Ten Commandments, expounded in the Sermon on the Mount and exemplified in Jesus Christ, that men are brought to cry out, "What must I do to be saved?" "Is not my Word like as a fire? saith the Lord; and like a hammer that breaketh a rock in pieces?" This does not mean that we are to thump and bash people on the head with a Bible like a sledgehammer. In Jamaica, the government employs women to break up rocks for use on the country roads. These women sit by the roadside, not blasting the rocks with one blow, but tapping them with a light hammer, over and over, again and again, until finally the rock gives along its flaw-line and falls to pieces. So God's Word, used firmly and persistently but gently, will break in pieces the hardest heart.

The Holy Spirit also uses to bring conviction the living of the Word of God in the church. The Lord Jesus Christ indicated this when he told his disciples that the world would hate them, just as it had hated him. Because the Christian did not belong to the world, but had been chosen by Christ out of the world, his life was a rebuke to the standards of the world, and therefore he would be rejected by it. " . . . all this they will do to you on my account, because they do not know him who sent me. If I had not come and spoken to them, they would not have sin; but now they have no excuse for their sin . . . If I had not done among them the works which no one else did, they would not have sin" (John 15: 21,22,24). Jesus obviously anticipated that just as his works and behavior among men had brought their sin to light and caused men to reject him, so there would also be a quality of life in his followers which would be an implicit condemnation of the sin of the world. How then can we expect the world to be convicted of its sin until they see a higher standard of holiness in the church? J. G. Machen said years ago, "If the consciousness of sin is to be produced, the Law of God must be proclaimed in the lives of Christian people as well as in word. It is quite useless for the preacher to breathe out fire and brimstone from the pulpit, if at the same time the occupants of the pews go on taking sin very lightly and being content with the moral standards of the world. The rank and file of the church must do their part in so proclaiming the Law of God by their lives that the secrets of men's hearts shall be revealed."[12]

The Holy Spirit also uses the praying of God's people to bring conviction of sin. Canon Bryan Green has noted, "Prayer meetings are dying out in our modern churches, and so is real conviction of sin—is it only a coincidence?" The preacher not only has a right to expect but a duty to demand of God's people that they pray for him, that he may be given utterance and speak as he ought to speak, not as a religious lecturer, but as a prophet of God and an ambassador of Christ (Ephesians 6:19,20). What added boldness the preacher may have when he knows that his people are lifting him up in prayer as he declares Christ and decries sin!

Most of all, the Holy Spirit uses the lifting up of the Lord Jesus Christ to produce the sense of our sin. Jesus spoke of the convicting work of the Holy Spirit in a threefold way, " . . . He will convince the world of sin and of righteousness and of judgment" (John 16:8). Consider these elements briefly. He is to convict the world of sin, to show the world that it completely needs to change its mind as to what sin is. What is the criterion of the world's sin? He will convince "of sin, because they do not believe in me," said Jesus (John 16:9). The fundamental sin of all is unbelief, and the Holy Spirit presses home to men this root sin in showing that the world's inexcusable rejection of Jesus Christ manifested its unbelief toward God. The Holy Spirit convicts the world "of righteousness, because I go to the Father . . . " (John 16:10). The world is just as ignorant of true goodness as it is of true sin. Would men bow down before goodness if they saw it incarnate? For the answer, look at Jesus Christ. He typified perfect righteousness, yet the world judged him to be a criminal and put him on a cross. But the resurrection and ascension of Christ—"I go to my Father"—show that God reversed the world's verdict and vindicated the righteousness of Christ.

He will convince the world "of judgment, because the ruler of this world is judged" (John 16:11). Sin chosen and righteousness refused must result in condemnation. The Holy Spirit convinces men that judgment is to come, because judgment has already come. What is the proof? Look again at the cross and the resurrection, and you see that God has turned man's judgment upside down. When the crucified Prince of Peace rose to his kingdom of righteousness, then the prince of this world fell in his kingdom of darkness. It is in relation to Jesus Christ that the Holy Spirit exposes sin, vindicates righteousness, and convinces of judgment.

Conviction came in Peter's sermon when he pointed to the cross and solemnly indicted the crowd: " . . . God has made him both Lord and Christ, this Jesus whom you crucified" (Acts 2:36). There comes a time when the evangelist, in all humility and love, must stop saying "we" and say "you."

Perhaps conviction is aroused more than any other way by picturing our responsibility in the crucifixion and how our sin hurt God. It was our cowardice, our greed, our compromise, our bigotry, our indifference that nailed him there. And as the Holy Spirit breaks us before that stark and cruel cross, amazingly, the hand that we crucified is stretched out to us—the burden rolls from our back—and from hearts contrite with true sorrow we rise to follow him who loved us and gave himself for us.

That is true conviction of sin. That is "godly sorrow which leads to repentance not to be repented of."

[1]D. Martyn Lloyd-Jones, *Studies in the Sermon on the Mount*, Vol. I (London: Inter-Varsity Christian Fellowship, 1959), p. 235.

[2]W. E. Sangster, *Let Me Commend* (London: The Epworth Press, 1961), p. 47.

[3]Karl Barth, *Church Dogmatics*, Vol. IV (Edinburgh: T. and T. Clark, 1956), p. 395.

[4]*Ibid.*, pp. 363-389.

[5]*Ibid.*, pp. 397-399.

[6]*Ibid.*, pp. 400-402.

[7]*Ibid.*, pp. 403-404.

[8]*Ibid.*, pp. 407-412.

[9]*Towards the Conversion of England* (London: The Press and Publications Board of the Church Assembly, 1945), p. 36.

[10]A. Paget Wilkes, *The Dynamics of Service* (London: Japan Evangelistic Band, 1955), pp. 88,79-80.

[11]J.I. Packer, *Evangelism and the Sovereignty of God* (London: Inter-Varsity Christian Fellowship, 1961), pp. 59-61.

[12]J.G. Machen, *Christianity and Liberalism* (Grand Rapids: Wm. B. Eerdmans, 1946), p. 67.

CHAPTER 9

The Place of Decision

THE last mark of Peter's sermon is this: It called for immediate and definite response. "And Peter said to them, "Repent, and be baptized every one of you in the name of Jesus Christ for the forgiveness of your sins; and you shall receive the gift of the Holy Spirit"(Acts 2:38).

The average pastor today would be rather shocked if the congregation cried out at the end of his sermon, "What shall we do?" His homiletics class would not very likely have prepared him for this situation! I can imagine a typical reply: "Well . . . let us all consider this very carefully to see if there is anything at all that one or the other of us would want to do now or some time in the future!"

Christian evangelistic preaching means preaching to a verdict. It is first the indicative mood: a declaration of what God has done. But it is also preaching in the imperative mood: a demand for what God commands man to do. Our Lord himself is our example here. " . . . Jesus came into Galilee, preaching the gospel of God, and saying, 'The time is fulfilled, and the kingdom of God is at hand; repent and believe in the gospel' "(Mark 1:14,15). Jesus constantly used the imperative. There was an urgency and immediacy— yet with a strong note of warning to count the cost—in his appeals. "Follow me . . . believe in me . . . come after me," he said, but also "take up your cross . . . forsake all that you have."

"Choose! Decide!" He was constantly demanding. Yes! Or

no!

"Our business," said James Black, "is serious gunfire with a target." Evangelism, says one definition of the World Council of Churches, means "so making Christ known to man that each is confronted with the necessity of a personal decision, Yes or No." This whole area of "decision" and "invitation" bristles with difficulties for many. All we can do is to touch a few of them.

There is the theological issue. Many preachers, such as the late Dr. Donald Gray Barnhouse and Dr. Martyn Lloyd-Jones, refuse to make any public invitation. They apparently feel a theological inconsistency between the doctrines of man's inability, of grace, of God's election, and such appeals. Their objection, of course, is not to spiritual decision and conversion, but rather to any method which may seem to put undue stress on the psychological aspects of decision. The whole question revolves around the issue of God's sovereignty and man's responsibility, or what God does as King and what he does as Judge.

There is a story told of a young man who came to the Scottish preacher, John McNeil. He was on the point of graduating from theological college and was deeply concerned, as he went out to preach, for fear he might offer free grace to some who were not of the elect. "Laddie," replied Dr. McNeil with a twinkle in his eye, "don't you be worried. If you should get the wrong man saved, the Lord will forgive you for it!" McNeil's practical good humor may be of more help than all the theological wrangling that has divided Calvinists and Arminians.

But we must recognize, as Packer has said, that there is a real antinomy in Scripture—not just a paradox, but an apparent incompatibility between these two doctrines. We cannot solve it. We must learn to live with it. And we must avoid the temptation either to an exclusive concern with human responsibility (which makes us panicky and alarmist), or to an exclusive concern with divine sovereignty (which can make us cynical about all evangelistic endeavors).[1]

There are plenty of biblical precedents for holding these two truths together. In Matthew 11:27 Jesus is recorded as saying, " . . . no one knows the Father except the Son and any one to whom the Son chooses to reveal him," but this did not prevent our Lord from giving in the very next verse this all-inclusive invitation: "Come to me, all who labor and are heavy laden, and I will give you rest." He put the two truths in one sentence in John 6:37: "All that the Father gives me will come to me; and him who comes to me I will not cast out." Paul's magnificent discussion of God's election in Romans 9 did not prevent him from having a great burden and yearning of heart. Indeed, he opens that very chapter with these words, "I am speaking the truth in Christ, I am not lying; my conscience bears me witness in the Holy Spirit, that I have great sorrow and unceasing anguish in my heart. For I could wish that I myself were accursed and cut off from Christ for the sake of my brethren, my kinsmen by race" (Romans 9:1-3).

If anyone feels that he cannot give an invitation for a sinner to come to Christ, because of man's inability, let him remember that Jesus invited a man whose hand was paralyzed to do what he could not do! " . . . Stretch out your hand . . . " Jesus commanded (Matthew 12:13), and the man obeyed the command and did what he could not do! Let him remember also that Jesus told the dead man to do something he could not do—to live! " . . . Lazarus, come forth," He commanded (John 11:43), and Lazarus obeyed the voice of Jesus and did what he could not do!

A friend of mine was discussing evangelism with a professor of theology. The professor, who is strongly sacramentarian in his emphasis, was objecting strenuously to evangelistic appeals as used in modern campaigns. He maintained that we must preach the Gospel and leave the matter there. My friend replied along this line, "Professor, you are always emphasizing to us the importance of the sacraments in the Christian life. Now, is it enough to display the wine and the bread on the Communion table, and to declare objectively that this stands for our Lord's broken body and poured-out blood? Of course it is not. We must also go on to give the invitation in Christ's place, 'Take, eat. Take, drink.' And this," went on my friend, "is what the evangelist is doing when he says, 'Come to Jesus.' "

What we must beware of is making our evangelistic appeal all imperative and no indicative, or else of so dividing between the indicative and the imperative that we give men the impression that God is responsible for 50 percent of our salvation and we for the other 50 percent. Salvation is "all of grace." We must beware of making a Christ out of our faith," declared Spurgeon. "The trembling hand can receive a golden gift." We are saved "by grace, through faith." It is grace that saves; it is faith that receives. And even that faith is " . . . not of yourselves, it is the gift of God" (Ephesians 2:8). God commands all men everywhere to repent and believe, but even when we make our decision, God does not leave us on our own. His grace is in his command, and his grace is in our response.

If I may add a personal word, I have discovered that faith in God's sovereign grace and salvation has helped me in two basic attitudes toward my evangelistic work. For one thing, it has kept me from losing heart, from pessimism. Only the sovereignty of God is sufficient ground for preaching to a verdict. Otherwise, evangelism is a hopeless task. We are told in Scripture that the "natural man does not receive the things of the Spirit of God . . . " (1 Corinthians 2:14). We learn that " . . . the carnal mind . . . is not subject to the law of God, neither indeed can be" (Romans 8:7). We are told that outside of Christ men are dead in trespasses and sins (Ephesians 2:1) and blinded by the god of this world (2 Corinthians 4:4). How can a dead man live and a blind man see? But with God all things are possible.

Ananias must have felt that Saul was a hopeless case, when the word came to him that he should go to this arch-persecutor of the church and lay his hands on him. Ananias protested, "Lord, I have heard from many about this man, how much evil he has done to thy saints at Jerusalem" (Acts 9:13). But the Lord said to him, "Go, for he is a chosen instrument of mine . . . " (Acts 9:15). Ananias said, "How much evil he has done—it is impossible that he be converted." God said, "He is a chosen vessel—it is not impossible with me."

But this confidence in God also guards us from self-dependence, from opportunism. There is a great danger in the success status psychology of our day. The pressure to produce results lies particularly heavy on the evangelist. But the pastor is also pushed to "get results" in our competitive society, which demands more members, better programs, and bigger attendance. This leads to trusting in techniques and manipulation, and brings the danger of leading people into premature, abortive decisions before they have really faced up to the meaning of the Gospel and the demands of the Christian life. The last state of this person is often worse than the first. God holds me responsible for "faithful evangelism" not for success. Therefore I may plead, but never coerce. Our pattern is Jesus, who never manipulated or forced people. When the rich young ruler came in his eagerness and went away sad, Jesus watched his retreating figure with an unutterable grief. But he did not run after him. He did not strong-arm his way into his life. He neither lowered his demands nor increased the pressure.

So must we, when we invite men to Christ, keep very close to the scriptural pattern and the biblical terminology, and invite men to come to God in the name of a Christ who is not a beggar but imperial Lord.

There is also the emotional issue in giving the invitation. The question of emotions in evangelism arises at this point as much or more than at any other. Many have reacted against all appeals, because they have been put off by experiences of invitations which have been given without taste, without tact, without dignity, and with a questionable emotional manipulation of people.

I think we must learn to distinguish between emotionalism and emotion. Emotionalism is emotion isolated, emotion for emotion's sake. There is a legitimate place for emotion in preaching the Gospel. Nothing truly human lacks emotion. If you think back to some experience that has left its imprint on you, there will certainly have been some deep and great emotion connected with it. In this whole matter of emotions we have tended to one of two extremes: to be overzealous or overcautious. By and large, the orthodox churches have been far too restrained. That is why many of the sect groups are growing so rapidly. As Dr. Mackay says, "Something is wrong when emotion becomes legitimate in everything except religion."

Two priceless quotes from a Tennessee mountain preacher put emotion in the right perspective. "Today we go to the football game" he says, "to do our shouting, to the movies to do our crying, and to church to do our freezing!" And he provides a good test of the reality of the emotional aspect of any experience when he says, "I don't care how high you jump, or how loud you shout, as long as when you hit the ground you walk straight!"

But we must recognize clearly the real danger involved in a decision that is primarily emotional in character. It is usually followed by a pendulumlike backward swing when hard realities challenge the emotional assurance. And this results either in a constant attempt to reproduce the emotional state, thus in an unbalanced Christian life; or in a feeling of betrayal and suspicion, and reaction against any religious experience at all.

The evangelist should remember that he is speaking to the whole man—intellect, conscience, emotion, will—and that God wants the response of the whole man. "Thou shalt love the Lord thy God with all thy heart, and with all thy soul, and with all thy mind, and with all thy strength . . . " (Mark 12:30).

There is to be an appeal to the intellect, a strong emphasis on teaching, in an evangelistic ministry. "Obey the truth"—that is how Paul again and again describes the response to the Gospel. Luke describes Paul's ministry, saying he "disputed" (Acts 9:29), or "reasoned" (Acts 17:2), or "taught" (Acts 18:11), or "persuaded" (Acts 18:4). But the evangelist also speaks to the conscience. " . . . commending ourselves to every man's conscience . . . " Paul said again (2 Corinthians 4:2). There is a type of evangelistic message which is 10 percent teaching and 90 percent appeal. This reverses the proportion of the New Testament. Through the avenues of intellect, conscience, emotion, we seek to reach the central citadel where a man will in his total personality say Yes to the Yes of God in Christ.

I am convinced that the giving of some kind of public invitation to come to Christ is not only theologically correct, but also emotionally sound. Men need this opportunity for expression. The inner decision for Christ is like driving a nail through a board. The open declaration of it is like clinching the nail on the other side, so that it is not easily pulled out. Impression without expression can lead to depression. Prof. William James said, "When once the judgment is decided let a man commit himself; let him lay on himself the necessity of doing more, let him lay on himself the necessity of doing all. Let him take a public pledge if the case allows. Let him envelop his resolution with all the aids possible."

To be sure, there are emotional dangers involved. People can respond to a hypercharged atmosphere, or to some pathetic story. So we must be careful that in the evangelistic presentation everything is so planned and carried out that it is the truth of the Word of God that stands central and supreme, and is the focus of attention. We must also be sure to warn people that the Christian life does not move on moods and thrills, but by trust and obedience. The initial moment of decision is a needed and helpful highlight, but it is no more the whole of the Christian life than the honeymoon is the whole of marriage. We must also warn people not to confuse emotional experience with spiritual reality. Our Lord spoke of the seed which sprang up quickly but had no root, and compared it to those who receive a sermon with joy but soon fade away. And we must remember that there will be some neurotic or disturbed persons who usually respond to such appeals and who need sensitive and expert counseling.

But having recognized the pitfalls I am still persuaded that the blessings of direct evangelism, which confronts people to a point of decision, far outweigh the perils.

Then there is the practical issue involved. The danger here is that of having no method of bringing people to Christ, or else of idolizing one method. We have got to beware of imagining that we can put the Holy Spirit in a box and dictate how everyone must come to Christ. Many seeking and believing souls have been frustrated for years because they have been unable to reproduce exactly the experience of conversion a friend went through.

A leading Baptist churchman once said that when he was converted at a camp meeting in his youth, he went forward and knelt at an old-fashioned altar. Someone came along and clapped him on one shoulder, saying "Brother, come and hold on." Another person hit him on the other shoulder and said, "Brother, come and let go!" The third man said, "When I was saved, a big light came from heaven and hit me right in the face." Said the preacher, "Between holding on, and letting go, and looking for the light, I almost missed the kingdom of God!"

Jesus healed many blind men during his ministry. And he healed each of them in a unique way. To one man, he simply said, "Receive your sight," and he saw. But for another man he mixed mud and put it on his eyes, and told him to go and wash it off. Now suppose those two men had met years later. One might have inquired of the other, "What did Jesus do for you?" The answer would be, "I was blind and Jesus made me see." "You don't say! Jesus gave me back my sight too. How did he heal you?" The second man would say, "He simply said for me to see, and my eyesight came." "He didn't put mud on your eyes? He didn't send you down to the river to wash it off? Why, man, you can't see at all! You're still blind!" And if they had been like our modern churches, they would have had two different denominations out of it : the Muddites and the "Anti-Muddites"!

No one method is suitable for every Sunday, every church, and every culture. I have preached in conservative churches or areas where people are very reserved, and have not felt it wise to ask people to come forward, particularly in a smaller meeting, but rather have asked them to remain behind or come to another room for counseling after the service. On the other hand, we have been in areas of the world where people are very free and unrestrained in the expression of their feelings, and everyone would flood forward in an open public invitation. In that situation, we have also asked people to remain behind and to seek counseling after the service. The truth is that some method or other is right everywhere. There are many approaches in inviting people to decision.

1. The invitation to come forward at the close of a sermon. The advantage of this method is that it is clear-cut and decisive. The disadvantage is that some will hold back because of shyness, or rebel because they regard it as unseemly or some sort of exhibitionism. After experimenting with many different approaches in many different situations, I have become convinced myself that in most instances the following approach is the best.

When a minister expects to give this invitation, it is wise to explain ahead of time, before or during his sermon, what he intends to do, and then build toward this moment of decision throughout the entire message. It is important that the invitation not be tacked on at the end as an afterthought. Neither should it be anti-climactic. It is a mistake for the preacher to build to a great height, closing with some powerful story, and then almost visibly let down as he says, "Now we invite you to come to Christ." The evangelistic sermon ought to move on a constantly ascending line as it comes to its climax, and a high moment ought to come when the preacher finishes his appeal and says, "Now come."

If you are going to give an invitation, prepare your invitation as you do the rest of your sermon. Think through clearly what you are going to say and do. Plan with the choir and the choir director your final hymn, and who will sing it, and whether or not you will pause after certain verses. Have a definite place prepared for counseling with those who come forward, whether in front of the sanctuary or auditorium, or in another room.

When you give the appeal, explain the reason you give it. Remember that the procedure is unfamiliar to many people. Explain it as a means of obeying Christ's command to confess him before men, and a step which will help to make the decision definite and clear-cut. Make the invitation as straightforward as possible. Avoid vague appeals which imply that everyone should come. If your object is to reach people who are making a first-time commitment to Christ, say so. If you are also including those who are coming back to Christ, or those who may want to come for assurance, say so.

I have found it helpful to speak of the symbolism involved in the invitation. It is an open sign of an inward decision. A man makes a promise, says in his heart "I'll keep my word," and shakes hands as a sign. A soldier sees the flag go by. In his heart, he says, "I'll be loyal to my country." He salutes—it is a sign. A young couple in their hearts commit themselves to each other and pledge their loyalty in the giving of self. And they stand at the front of the church and pledge themselves openly, in word and in kiss. It is a visible sign of their inward commitment. So when people come from their seats and stand at the front, it is an open sign that, as they come with their feet to the front, so they are coming with their hearts to Jesus Christ.

Deception must by all means be avoided. Each man must be convinced in his own heart, but I feel there is danger in asking people to go through several steps; first to raise their hand, then to stand, then to come forward. Some people will raise a hand who would have no intention of going forward, and if they did so would later feel that they had been tricked and betrayed. It is far better to explain clearly and ask people to take just one step. It is also important to tell people what will happen to them after they come forward, especially for the sake of strangers and those who are not familiar with invitations. I have known of people who have been afraid to come forward to "confess Christ" because they think this means they will go into a counseling room and have to confess their sins publicly. When you give the appeal say, "After you have come forward, we would like to have a prayer with you and give you a further word of instruction about the Christian life, to have some counseling with you and to answer your questions, to give you some literature which will help you to read your Bible and to go on in the Christian life, and then you may go or rejoin your friends." What will happen should be clearly explained before, not after people have come forward.

2. The "after-service." In some cases, it may be wise to ask those who want to make their decision or inquire further about Christian commitment to remain behind, or go to another room after the main service. The advantage of this is that it gives people time to think and reaches some shy folk who could never bring themselves to come forward. The disadvantage is that it is not quite as decisive and allows an "out" to some who might have come forward. But, after all, our trust is not in the method but in the Lord. He who convicts the heart in the first place is surely able to bring men to himself in his way.

The pattern for an after-service varies widely, but it is a method which has been used successfully for many years. Evangelists such as D. L. Moody and Dr. R. A. Torrey made much more use of an after-service than of the invitation to come forward.

In leading up to an after-service, one might say something like this: "At the end of the sermon tonight, I am going to lead in a brief prayer. Following the prayer, there will be an opportunity for those of you who wish to leave, or must leave to do so. Then we are going to have a brief after-meeting for all of you who can remain, in which I am going to state as clearly as I know how the steps in coming to Jesus Christ. I hope that all of you who can will stay. If you are not a Christian and you wish to become a Christian, please stay. If you are not sure and you wish to make sure, I invite you to stay. If you are not prepared yet to come to Christ, but you want to know more about it, you are welcome to stay. If you are already committed to Christ, I hope that you will stay to encourage others. The fact that you stay does not mean that you are not a Christian. The fact that you go, if you wish to or must, does not mean that you are not interested. If you do stay, no one will approach you or embarrass you in any way. The after-service will not last more than ten minutes."

Dismiss with a brief prayer, ask the organist or pianist to play quietly, and give an opportunity for those who are leaving to do so quickly and quietly. Ask the ushers then to close the doors. If the remaining crowd is scattered, you may wish to ask them all to come toward the front, and to go down and speak to them from the floor of the church or auditorium.

At this point I have usually asked people to bow in a moment of silent prayer, asking God to speak to them. I then give as clearly and as concisely as possible the steps in becoming a Christian (as outlined below). Often I have asked those who wish to make this decision to repeat silently after me a prayer of commitment and then to raise their hands as a sign if they have made a decision. I then explain the importance of confessing Christ openly, and ask those who have made the decision and have so indicated to come and tell me of their decision at the close of the after-service; to take a card which they will sign as an affirmation of their faith; and to receive some literature and, if possible, personal counseling. Then the after-service is dismissed with a benediction. It is most important that the after-service be promptly concluded within the time limits announced.

3. Instruction in the counseling room or after-service. Whether

you are speaking to inquirers who have come forward at an invitation, or to people who have remained behind for an after-service, it is important to put them at ease by a warm but reverent attitude. I believe this is especially important when inquirers have been taken to another room, for many are wondering what will be done to them. It may be wise to say, "We welcome you friends in the name of Christ. Perhaps you are wondering just what we are going to do to you, and how you will ever get out of here, if you get out! Well, I want to assure you that we are not going to do anything to you, or put you through a 'third degree.' You are not going to be embarrassed, and you don't have to make a speech. We wanted to have this chance to share something more of the meaning of the Christian life, to have a prayer of commitment together, and to help you in going on with Christ."

At this point, some clear explanation needs to be made of how to come to Christ. While we want to avoid hackneyed expressions and stereotyped formulas, I have felt it vital to present these basic truths in an easily remembered fashion. The Gospel may be presented in terms of the "three R's"—in coming to Christ we must recognize our need, be prepared to renounce our sin, and to receive Christ. Or we may speak of the "A,B,C,D's": there is something to admit—that I have sinned, that I cannot save myself, that I need a Savior; there is something to believe—that Jesus Christ is the Savior and that he is able and willing to save me; there is something to consider—the cost of becoming a Christian, that Jesus is not only to be Savior but also my Lord; and there is something to do—I am not only to believe about Christ, but I am to entrust myself to him, in terms of Revelation 3:20: I not only believe that he wants to come in, but I open the door of my life and I ask him in.

The fourteenth and fifteenth verses of the first chapter of Mark make an excellent summary of Christian decision. " . . . Jesus came into Galilee, preaching the Gospel of God, and saying, 'The time is fulfilled, and the kingdom of God is at hand; repent, and believe in the Gospel.' And passing along by the Sea of Galilee, he saw Simon and Andrew the brother of Simon casting a net in the sea; for they were fishermen. And Jesus said to them, 'Follow me, and I will make you become fishers of men.' " It can be pointed out that first of all Jesus declared something that God had done, and then he demanded something that men must do. This demand is found in three imperatives: (1) Repent. (2) Believe the Gospel. (3) Follow me. To repent not only means that I acknowledge I have sinned, not only that I am sorry about it, but that I change my mind about sin, and about God, and about myself—I am ready for God to change my life, and to leave my sin. To believe the Gospel not only means to give mental assent, but to give commitment of the will. I may believe there is a glass of water and know that I am thirsty, but the water will not help me unless I drink it. And Jesus calls us, knowing that when we do believe, the result will be a life of service. "Follow me," he says.

This explanation of becoming a Christian may be considered in terms of the great biblical word "Come." This is especially appropriate when people have come forward out of a crowd to the front, as a symbol of their coming to Jesus Christ. How do we come to Christ? We come humbly, knowing that we have sinned. The only person for whom Jesus can do nothing is a man who thinks he is so good that he needs nothing. The three hardest words in the English language to say, and really mean them, are, "I have sinned." But when I come to Jesus I come humbly, knowing my sin and being willing to turn from it. When I come to Jesus, I come in faith. How do I know that if I come he will receive me? I know because of the cross. There God says that he has taken care of my sin, that Christ has borne it for me. And there is God's promise, no matter what I have done or been, that it is all right to come home. He wants me to come. When I come to Christ, I come in surrender. I am not only asking him to forgive my past, and someday to take me to heaven, but I am coming to follow him here and now. He came to save me not only from my sins but for his service. I am deciding not merely to make one decision, but to enter into a life of decision in which I will daily come to Jesus Christ as my Lord.

Such explanation leads naturally into a prayer of commitment. In large Crusades, we often do this as a group prayer with all those who have come forward, for practical reasons. But I much prefer to have the inquirer pray personally, in the company of some trained and qualified counselor. This makes it possible for the prayer to be much more personal, and more in line with particular needs and the specific decisions about them which that person is making. Sometimes, when a small group has come to an after-service or to a counseling room in a church, after explaining the way to Christ, I have asked each member of the group to pray just one sentence out loud, according to their particular decision, whether it be rededication, assurance, or first-time commitment—even suggesting a sentence that they might pray, such as "Lord Jesus, come into my heart," or "I thank you for dying for me," or "I want you to be Lord of all. I dedicate my life to you."

Whether in a group or individually, the inquirer is sometimes shy and needs some guidance as to what to pray. So it is often helpful to lead in a prayer and ask the inquirer(s) to repeat the prayer out loud phrase by phrase after you. Prayer should be quite simple and direct, perhaps as follows: "Oh God, I come to you today, as best I know how. I come to you humbly, for I know that I have sinned, and I want to turn from my sin. I come to you in faith, for I believe Christ loved me and died for me. I do trust him now as my Savior. Come into my heart, Lord Jesus. I come to you in surrender. Take my life and help me to follow you, in your church, and in my daily life. I thank you for receiving me. In Jesus' name. Amen."

There are two things which are very important to stress with any inquirer. One is the matter of assurance. We need to distinguish between the sense of relief, which may be based on temporary emotion, and permanent assurance which is based on conviction brought by the Holy Spirit from the never-changing Word of God. Often in speaking to someone who has "made a decision" I have asked if they knew now that they belonged to Christ and that he was in their heart, and the answer has come, "Oh yes. I feel so clean. I feel as if a burden has been lifted. I feel a great joy." Now we ought not to criticize nor belittle such feelings. Emotional experiences are a genuine part of coming to Christ, and there is joy and peace in believing. What we need to do is to point out that such feelings do not always come immediately to the new convert, and they certainly do not always last. There will come times of pressure, of doubt, and of temptation, when the convert will question the reality of his relationship with Christ. Then he needs to have far more than a feeling on which to base his faith.

I often take a simple verse of Scripture, such as John 1:12, or John 6:37, or Revelation 3:20, and ask the inquirer to read that verse carefully. I then ask if they have fulfilled the condition—if they have received Christ, or come to him, or opened the door to him—and if the answer is "Yes," then go on to ask if they now are the child of God, if Christ has received them, if he has come into their heart. Very often the answer will be, "Well, I think so," or "I hope so." I then hold out a New Testament, or a pencil, and say, "If I told you I was going to give this to you tomorrow, and you went home and told someone that you were going to get a gift tomorrow, and they asked how you knew, what would you reply?" The obvious answer is, "Leighton Ford told me." How could you be sure of it? "Because I can trust you." Well, can you trust God? Has he told you that he will receive you, save you, come into your life? And has he done it? How do you know? Because God says so. This point needs to be made over again and again and again, and if necessary again and again, until the inquirers see—and often it will burst in with a glorious light upon their souls—that their relationship with Christ does not depend on what they have done, and on what they feel. But it depends on what he has done, and on what he says.

Great discernment is necessary at this point, of course. We do not want to give false assurance to the person who is resisting the Holy Spirit and who is holding back from receiving Christ. We must not seek to bring assurance prematurely, before the issues of salvation by grace through faith, of repentance from sin, of commitment to discipleship have been faced. But to the honest soul, who has sincerely accepted Christ, we can then point to this blessed assurance and pray that the Holy Spirit will witness in their hearts to the truth of the Word.

We need equally to stress that the decision for Christ is only the beginning. It is a beginning of pilgrimage, not an end. It is like the gun that starts a race. Like a new-born baby, the inquirer needs spiritual food in order that he may grow. The importance of Bible reading, of daily prayer, of fellowship and service in the church, of sharing Christ with others by the witness of life and conversation, should be underlined. Not as arbitrary rules but as the means of letting Jesus Christ pour his life into ours, and through ours to others. The Christian life may be pictured as a wheel, with Christ as the hub at the center, and the rim being the Christian coming into contact with the world about him. The spokes of the wheel—the Word of God, prayer, witnessing, obedience, fellowship—are the means by which the power of Christ keeps the Christian moving.

Those who wish further assistance in preparing personal counselors to help inquirers in evangelistic meetings, may wish to write the Billy Graham Evangelistic Association, 1300 Harmon Place, Minneapolis, MN 55403. Tape-recorded copies of the lectures used in training counselors for the Billy Graham Crusades, plus lecture notes and Bible studies for inquirers, are available.

4. Other methods of invitation. A wide variety of methods have

been used by different pastors and evangelists. Tom Rees, the British lay evangelist, closes his meetings with an "act of witness," as he calls it, and asks all those who have received Christ in the last two years to take part in it. This provides a helpful opportunity for public witness to many who have privately or in some other service committed their lives to Christ.

Dr. Ronald Ward, the Anglican evangelist, has a card placed in the pews in a church where he is conducting a mission. On this card is printed a statement of acceptance of Christ or of dedication of life. During a period of meditation at the close of his sermon, he will ask the congregation to take up the card and request those who are prepared to make their decision to fill it in and then take it with them after the benediction to another room, where they have a period of counseling.

We have used a variation on this in some of our Crusades, distributing to everyone at the beginning of the service a card which requests further information on how to become a Christian, or how to have assurance of salvation. We then ask those who have not come forward at the conclusion of the service, but would like more information, to fill in the card and leave it in a box at the door, or send it in to our office by mail. A helpful booklet is then sent to them, and where possible a counselor calls on them personally at their home to speak with them further.

Alan Walker, the Australian Methodist, has found it helpful during his invitation at his Sunday evening theater services in Sydney, to have certain specified counselors walk to the front of their aisle during each verse of the hymn of invitation, and then to guide those who come forward during the singing of that verse to the counseling room. Some churches will ask elders or deacons to come and stand at the front during the invitation, as a means of encouraging those who wish to make their decision.

An interesting letter from Conrad Thompson, a Lutheran secretary of evangelism, describes the methods which some Lutherans are using in their missions. He encourages the pastors to spend some time on one of the evenings explaining the various types of decisions to which the Holy Spirit leads people—both Christians and non-Christians.

Then an invitation is given for anyone who would like to come to the altar and kneel and meet his God privately there. Hundreds of Lutheran churches, he reports, have done this again and again. And thousands of their people have gone to kneel and to rededicate their lives to Christ, or to give their hearts to him at that time. An even more popular consecration service is the reiteration of the Confirmation vows. In this they ask the same questions that they do in the Confirmation service, except that the people are asked to answer in silence. At the conclusion of the questions the leader says, "There is one part of the service which was purposely left out. It is this, 'Give me your hand in token thereof.' Tonight, we are going to ask all of you to leave by way of the center aisle through one door, and all of you shake hands with your pastor. Some of you may be led by God to place your hand in the hand of your pastor and say, 'I will,' as evidence of your commitment to Jesus Christ tonight." Many Lutheran pastors, Thompson claims, have said that this has been the high point in their entire ministry. He also describes a number of other ideas used, such as the testimony meeting, the Communion service, and the confession of sin in private absolution service from the liturgy as people come to the altar and kneel. He concludes, "I do not want to give the impression that this is a mass movement in the Lutheran Church, but it has been multiplied tremendously in the last several years."

Among young people, the "say-so" meeting and the "fireside service" have been very helpful. The former is exactly what it implies—an informal meeting at the end of a conference or week of services, during which the young people who have made some commitment to Jesus Christ are asked to say so—to share briefly and concisely before the group what Christ has come to mean to them. The "fireside service" takes place around a fire, and those who have made a decision for Christ are asked to come and take a stick from a pile and place it on the fire as a symbol that their lives are being given to Christ as fuel for his fire in the world. They may also be asked to express briefly the meaning of their decision.

5. The "guest service." There are some congregations which, because of their size or location, or their tradition, find it effective to give some kind of invitation at almost every service. But there are many churches where an invitation given at every service loses its spontaneity, expectancy, and effectiveness, and becomes just an ineffectual—sometimes even boring—piece of ritual. There are other churches which, because of their background and tradition, would not feel comfortable with an invitation given at every service.

In such a situation a "guest service" may provide the answer.

This custom has been followed particularly in many of the evangelical Anglican churches in England and Australia. One Sunday morning or evening a month is set aside as a "guest service," and the whole congregation knows when it will be held. It may also be widely advertised in the community. At this particular service, the minister will give a clear-cut evangelistic address aimed at bringing people to Christian decision. Christian people will bring to this service their friends and neighbors whom they are seeking to win for Christ and his church. At the conclusion of the sermon an invitation will given, or an after-service held as described above.

6. The overtones of the invitation. The inner attitude of the evangelist or pastor, and the expression of it in the manner of giving the invitation are crucial. I personally have found it very helpful to study Billy Graham, for God has given him a unique gift in calling people to Christ. This is not merely the combination of his fine personality and excellent preaching, and most certainly cannot be explained as crowd psychology. I am convinced rather that it grows from the inner yearning of his heart. Joe Blinco, a former member of the Billy Graham team, tells how he was preaching in Adelaide, Australia, when Mr. Graham came in and sat at the rear of the auditorium (for he was to preach the following night). At the conclusion of the service, he came to Mr. Blinco and said, "Joe, that was a wonderful sermon. And you know at the end when you gave the invitation, I felt something welling up inside me. I wanted to stand up and ask the people to come to Christ." How many of us would have felt the same yearning, if we had not been preaching a sermon?

If God leads you to give an invitation, give it with conviction—a conviction that God is calling you to do this, that you are not doing it just to conform to what people expect. Give it with courage. Be prepared to risk embarrassing failure. Even if no one responds to the invitation, it is good to give it because it emphasizes the decisiveness which is involved in following Christ. Give it with compassion, humility, and gentleness. We are not inviting people to Christ out of a superiority complex, but as beggars telling other beggars where to get bread. William Temple said, "It is quite futile saying to people: 'Go to the cross.' We must be able to say: 'Come to the cross.' And there are only two voices which can issue that invitation with effect. One is the voice of the sinless Redeemer, with which we cannot speak; and one is the voice of the forgiven sinner, who knows himself forgiven. That is our part."[2]

Give it with urgency and definiteness. Don't be wishy-washy. The invitation should not be, "If there is anyone here who might want to come, you could come, or you could wait and see me afterward." Let it rather be: "God is calling. Come now. Come here." Give it with expectancy. "According to your faith, be it unto you," said Jesus. If we do not believe anything is going to happen, it will not. Give it with absolute integrity. Make the implications clear-cut. Don't be guilty of saying, "We shall sing only one more verse," and then singing fifteen more. Give it with empathy. Take up the desires, the fears, the questions, the hesitations and longings, of those who are deciding. Take time between some of the verses to express some of their questions, and to give brief answers to them. Do this with simplicity and straightforwardness. Don't confuse people with a multitude of instructions as to why and how they should come. Make your explanations as concise as you can.

There remains much room for deep thinking and wide experimentation in the church today in this matter of invitations. Dr. Helmut Thielicke, famed German preacher and theologian, sent a most moving letter to Billy Graham after he had attended the Crusade in Los Angeles. "I saw them all coming towards us, I saw there their assembled, moved, and honestly decided faces, I saw their searching and meditativeness. I confess that this moved me to the very limits. Above all there were two young men—white and Negro—who stood at the front and about whom one felt that they were standing at that moment on Mount Horeb and looking from afar into a land that they had longed for. I shall never forget those faces. It became lightning clear that men want to make a decision, and that the meditative conversation which we have cultivated in Germany since the war is only a poor fragment. I shall have to draw from all this certain consequences in my own preaching, even though the outward form will, of course, look somewhat different."

An English theological student was once sent by a professor to hear a noted preacher on the weekend. He came back with the sophisticated disgust that theological students sometimes affect, and said, "Why, that man didn't do anything but say, 'Come to Jesus'!" "And did they come?" his professor gently asked. "Well, yes, they did," came his grudging reply. "I want you to go back," said the professor, "and listen to that man preach again and again, until you can say, 'Come to Jesus' as he did, and people come.'"

And may God grant that we in the church today may go back

and listen to Peter again and again, until we so speak of Christ from the Scriptures that men are convinced and moved, and come to him.

[1]J.I. Packer, *Evangelism and the Sovereignty of God* (London: Inter-Varsity Christian Fellowship, 1961), Chap. 2.

[2]*Towards the Conversion of England* (London: The Press and Publications Board of the Church Assembly, 1945), p. 66.

CHAPTER 10

Is Evangelism Relevant?

WHEN Billy Graham appeared on "Town Meeting of the Air" a decade ago, a rather skeptical interrogator inquired, "Mr. Graham, if all the people in America were to be suddenly 'converted' according to your way of looking at conversion, in what way would that affect, say, the war that is going on in Korea?"

'Isn't evangelism really irrelevant," the question implied, "in the face of the staggering problems of the modern world?"

To many modern observers evangelism seems like an antique chair in a museum: a curious relic of the past and an interesting phenomenon for study, but not to be sat on, not fit to bear the weight of today's burdens—a hopeless anachronism in the twentieth-century world.

What is the use, ask such critics, of a church on its knees praying for lost souls, while a blinding population explosion dooms 100,000 new babies every day to slow starvation? What good is it for a vast throng to jam a stadium and listen to a sermon, while red-raw festering wounds of racial hatred blister the hide of civilization? Isn't it worse than futile to take a man into a corner and ask if he's "saved," while a terrifying arms race spawns mass terror weapons? Evangelism seems a ridiculous—yes, downright dangerous—misdirecting of our energies.

Even some Christians have had their zeal for evangelism hamstrung by these doubts. They wonder whether, as W. E. Sangster put it, "an aspirin as a cure for cancer would be less ridiculous than evangelism as the answer to the world's present ills. The human situation is so urgent. Talk of 'world revolution by individual conversion' is like talking about a long endowment policy to a man sitting on a time bomb."[1] Is evangelism really relevant amidst the tangled complexities of our modern dilemma?

Let me confess at the outset that I make no pretense of being objective. I write as a committed Christian and a committed evangelist. "Is evangelism relevant?" My answer is a resounding Yes! When people inquire as to the relevance of our Gospel, we must not be tricked into going on the defensive. We must immediately take the offensive, for our Lord himself has promised that the gates of hell shall not withstand the assault of his church. In this light, we need to rethink the question itself.

First, we need to define the subject of this question. "Is evangelism relevant?" really means "Is the evangel relevant?" For the genius of Christian evangelism is not in its method but in its message. There are many "evangelistic" techniques. Communism has its brainwashing; Islam its proselytism; the commercial world its hidden persuaders. But the relevance of Christian evangelism really concerns not its means, but its content. The message of evangelism is simply—Jesus Christ. Christian evangelism does not depend on any given technique; but it does depend on one given message—that God was in Christ reconciling the world unto himself. So when we ask, "Is evangelism relevant?" we are really asking, "Is Jesus Christ relevant?'

Second, we need to determine the thrust of this question, "Is evangelism relevant?" Relevant for what? And for whom? I was asked recently to engage in a panel TV discussion on the topic "Is Religion the Answer?" My answer was blunt: No! And I answered No because the question itself involved a misunderstanding of our real situation before God. Certainly Christ is the answer to ultimate questions! But our man-centered, earth-centered outlook tries to put God, as it were, "on the spot"! It is as if we present God with certain problems, grant him a polite hearing, and then if he can supply reasonable solutions, we consider the possibility of taking his advice. The whole idea is absurd! It is God who is asking the questions. From the beginning of Scripture, God addresses men and demands their response, calls to Adam, "Where art thou?" and to Cain, "Where is Abel, thy brother?" Is evangelism relevant? Again we ask, for what? Our purposes or God's?

The charge that Jesus Christ is irrelevant is not new. Indeed, people made the same accusation during his lifetime. John in his gospel tells of a great crowd which followed Jesus because they had seen his miracles, and says that he took some loaves and fishes from a little boy and fed the multitude with this tiny lunch. Because the people did not understand this sign, they tried to seize Jesus and make him king by force. But when Jesus realized their plan he withdrew to the hills by himself.

It is noteworthy that Jesus declined to be king on their terms. If he had wished to, he could have begun at that very moment a popular uprising against the Roman forces of occupation. But he refused to be "relevant." Why? As William Barclay has commented, "They wished to use him for their own purposes and to mold him to their own dreams. They looked for a messiah who could be king and conqueror, who would set his foot upon the eagle's neck and drive the Romans from Palestine, who would change Israel from a subject nation to a world power."[2]

"What a king he'd make," thought the crowd. "Let's harness his power to our plans and purposes." That attitude still lingers. We want Christ's gifts without his cross. We want to use Christ instead of allowing him to use us. Our humanistic, man-centered age habitually thinks more of what we want than of what God wants. The real question is not, "Is Jesus Christ relevant to us?" but, "Are we relevant to the purposes of Christ?"

Third, we need to decide the perspective from which we can answer this question. Our personal commitments are involved. A southern historian once wrote what he called "an unbiased history of the Civil War from the southern point of view"! If a man does not believe in God, nothing we can say is going to convince him that evangelism matters. The man who is opposed to the Gospel because he realizes its disturbing claims on his life cannot be neutral. He has a built-in hostility. Only the Holy Spirit can make evangelism relevant to him.

Much of the talk of making Christianity relevant is two thousand years old. Like the crowd who followed Jesus because they ate their fill of the loaves, but were not interested in "the food which endures to eternal life," the ungodly man assumes that nothing is relevant unless it gives first place to the material. The secularist says we no longer need God to fill the gaps in our knowledge; the Communist, that religion is an opiate; the sophisticate, that faith is fine for children but excess baggage for grown-ups. But what man thinks is relevant and what is really relevant to God may be very different things. Repentance, regeneration, and conversion mean a change of attitude and an inversion of values, without which men will still follow the mob that acclaimed Jesus when he offered them bread for their stomachs, but when he talked about eternal life, murmured, "This fellow isn't relevant any more," and went on looking for a more popular prophet.

It is only the man who has fed his hungry soul on Christ, the Bread of Life, who appreciates his true relevance and is able, like Peter, to answer Jesus' poignant question, "Will you also go away?" with a firm, "Lord, to whom shall we go? You have the words of eternal life."

Even the committed Christian has a problem in getting the whole picture. Eternity is the only adequate perspective from which to view the relevance of evangelism, because there are eternal issues at stake. In evangelism, we have to walk by faith and not by sight. We must evangelize not because we can see our success and prove our relevance, not because we can ferret out all the implications of our witness today for personal and social life tomorrow, but because our Lord Jesus Christ, himself the great Master Strategist, commands us to do so, and we believe that he will not let his Word return void.

History is helpful here. Looking back, we can see how God has blessed his Word in a way that would have been obscure to the people of a past age. What would the critics have said if they had seen that Jewish carpenter preaching from a boat and hanging from a cross? Would they have guessed that he, and not the Roman legions, would be the "hinge of history"?

Can you imagine how contemptuously they would have dismissed Paul's preaching in Athens? Could they have guessed that the message he preached would smash paganism and turn the Parthenon itself into a Christian church for centuries to come?

Which event would they have picked as most relevant in the early years of the fifth century: Alaric's sacking the city of Rome in 410, or Augustine's writing of *The City of God* in 413? Yet it was the bishop's book not the barbarian's bands, that controlled the Middle Ages.

Suppose they had lived in eighteenth-century England while revolution was brewing across the Channel and threatening in their own land, and had heard John Wesley preaching in a field. They would have cried, "Come down to earth! Problems enough here. Forget heaven. Be relevant." But Lecky has said that the Wesleyan revival saved England from the French Revolution.

If we are tempted to think our Gospel is too puny for this spin-
ning age of space and new revolutions, then let us remember that
Paul and Augustine and Wesley were relevant because they preached
Christ—and Christ is always relevant.

The evangelists of yesterday worked in a climate of public opinion far different from what we face. When Edwards, Finney, or
Moody preached, they knew that—with the exception of the occa-
sional "infidel"—the vast majority of those they sought to reach
believed in God, in sin, in hell, in heaven. Today, however, the
evangelist must communicate the Gospel to many spiritual illiterates.
The familiar evangelistic vocabulary is often meaningless to these
people, and—even more important—the traditional evangelistic concerns of salvation, forgiveness, and eternal life are remote from
their daily life. How do we reach these spiritual aliens? In his book
What Is Evangelism? Canon Douglas Webster points out that these
"outsiders" to whom the church seems irrelevant fall into two main
classes: the intellectual man and the industrial man.[3]

The intellectual man, from one standpoint, is characterized
by despair, as typified by the existentialist, the beatnik, or the angry
young man. For him, God is dead. Life is meaningless, an "in-
definite waiting for an explanation that never comes," as in Samuel
Beckett's play *Waiting for Godot.*

John Osborne, one of the leaders of Britain's angry young men,
expresses this in his play *Look Back in Anger* through the blunt
words of Jimmy Porter: "I suppose people of our generation aren't
able to die for good causes any longer. We had all that done for
us, in the 30's and 40's, when we were still kids. There aren't any
good brave causes left. If the big bang comes, and we all get killed off, it won't be in aid of the old-fashioned grand design. It'll
just be for the Brave, New Nothing-very-much-thank-you. About
as pointless and inglorious as stepping in front of a bus."[4]

On the other hand, paradoxically, intellectual man feels that
his new religion of scientism answers his problems of material existence. "Man has learned," reflected Dietrich Bonhoeffer in his
Nazi cell, "to cope with all questions of importance without
recourse to God as a working hypothesis . . . it is becoming evident that everything gets along without 'God' and just as well as
before."[5] Bonhoeffer took evangelism to task for relying on a sort
of "God of the Gap," a God whom we call in to account for those
gaps in our knowledge which science cannot yet explain, or to solve

our personal problems.

Bonhoeffer may have exaggerated the situation, but his warning should give us pause. Here, for example, is a young engineer. He is happily married. His company has made him financially secure. Scientific training at the university has convinced him that most questions can be satisfactorily answered by scientific methods, and those that cannot be so answered are not worth asking. His moral exterior is impeccable. He is a fine father, a useful citizen, and finds real fulfillment in his work. He drinks, but moderately, and is not beset by sexual temptations. In short, he seems to be well-balanced and happy, enjoying life with no great sense of need. Perhaps this is drawing too perfect a picture. But if this man says he feels no need of Christ, how do I persuade him otherwise? "Pray for him" says someone. And indeed, we should. "Only God can make him feel his need," says someone else. I agree. But the point is that God does not usually speak to men in a vacuum. "How shall they hear without a preacher?" God expects me to witness to such men. In what way can I present Jesus Christ so that the Gospel may impinge on his life?

The industrial man is also, by and large, a lost frontier for the Gospel. This is more evident today in western Europe than North America. But most labor union adherents in the United States and Canada are far beyond the sphere of evangelical influence.

In contrast to the intellectual, Douglas Webster suggests that "industrial society presents an entirely different kind of man—mass man, organization man, man deprived of much scope for individual initiative or individual reponsibility." Mass man watches the same TV programs, reads the same newspapers, attends the same movies, goes through the same schools as all his fellows. He becomes man without personality.

Can evangelism be made relevant to intellectual man with his existentialist despair and scientific confidence, and to industrial man with his mass response and materialistic preoccupation?

J. B. Phillips took a group of English young people and asked them to give their immediate response to a series of questions. One was, "Do you think God understands radar?" Eighteen out of twenty put down "No" as their first reaction. Then they laughed as the absurdity of their answer hit them! Of course God understands radar! But subconsciously they were relegating God to the nineteenth century.

Twentieth-century man may live in a new culture, but his basic anxieties are ageless. The fear of nuclear catastrophe has served to expose rather than to create this malaise. It comes in part from the strain of living in a disheveled, revolutionary world, but grows ultimately from a deep spiritual dislocation. Philosophers such as Tillich have spoken of three types of human anxiety: the anxiety of death, the anxiety of guilt, the anxiety of emptiness and meaninglessness. What is more relevant to such anxieties than the Gospel?

Take the anxiety of death. Even the modern pagan, trying to live within the horizons of a sensual world, cannot ignore death. He may scoff at judgment beyond, but he cannot escape the anxiety of knowing that some day this life—the only life he knows—will be cut off forever. One thinks of the famous publisher who never allowed death to be mentioned in his presence. One thinks of the weird cults that draw the morbid with their promised insights into the world beyond. In giving a reason for our hope of eternal life, the Christian evangelist has no lack of relevant material.

Or take the anxiety about guilt. Guilt and forgiveness cannot be cavalierly dismissed in this neurotic day as once they were. Dr. O. Hobart Mowrer, the famed research professor of psychology at the University of Illinois, though by no means an evangelical, has recently in the Atlantic Monthly called for a rediscovery of moral responsibility, and in effect criticized psychoanalysis for its loss of the concept of sin.

Graham Greene dramatically portrays the nemesis of guilt in his novel *The Quiet American*. His central character, a blasé cynical English journalist in the Far East, has been responsible for the death of a young American who was threatening the journalist's security by trying to marry his Asian mistress. The novel's last paragraph describes the Englishman's belated remorse. The man has no religion to provide absolution, and yet he says, "I wish there were someone that I could tell how sorry I am."

Donald Baillie asked, "Why is it such maladies as 'nervous breakdowns' are so common in our modern world? Is it entirely unconnected with the fact that there are now so many serious-minded people who have no belief in God, who are trying to have morality without religion? Because they have no God, they have no saving secret for dealing with their moral failures. Their memory of failure, instead of becoming a wholesome sense of sin which can lead to forgiveness, is unconsciously repressed until it becomes a morbid complex, with paralyzing effects."[6] It was also Dr. Baillie who quoted the testimony of an Edinburgh psychiatrist: "I always send my patients to hear Dr. X preach, because he preaches the doctrine of the forgiveness of sins."

The message of the cross, we see, is by no means passé. It alone is radical enough to plumb the depths of guilt. It answers three great questions. Is forgiveness necessary? Yes, we answer, look at Jesus on the cross! There most clearly we see the curse of sin. Is forgiveness possible? Yes, we answer, look at Jesus on the cross! His blood shed for us is pledge of God's love to the sinner. But is forgiveness just? Yes, we answer again, look at Jesus on the cross! God did not make light of sin. Rather, the Judge allowed himself to be judged in our place to transform us by his grace.

Let the message go out, then, to a guilt-laden world that "in him there is redemption through his blood"!

But what about the third anxiety—that of meaninglessness? If, as has been suggested, anxiety about death especially characterized ancient civilizations, and anxiety about guilt predominated in the Middle Ages and throughout the Reformation, this third anxiety is certainly especially true of us today.

Modern man may pretend not to give much thought to death and what lies beyond. He may picture himself as a pretty good fellow, not as a lost sinner before a holy God. But he is often prepared to acknowledge that he is "lost" in that he is wandering, aimless, and empty.

Modern life testifies to this emptiness. Think of the proliferating symptoms of our jaded, banal lives: the forests of TV antennas— the multitudes vicariously identifying themselves with every escapade of the Hollywood star—the lust for status symbols—the pep pills and tranquilizers—the frantic rush to keep up with the Joneses. They all bespeak an emptiness, a soul that cries for the water of life.

The scientist finds that his laboratory can supply no clues to ultimate value. The organization man discovers that security without commitment looks futile in middle age. The mass man senses that his collective herd reactions fail to satisfy his longing to be recognized as an individual.

Modern psychiatry testifies to this meaninglessness. Here are the comments of just a few noted psychiatrists. Dr. Rollo May has said that the main problem with most of the patients who come to him in the middle of the twentieth century is a "vague sense of undirectedness." Carl Jung claimed that "the central neurosis of our time is emptiness." Dr. Erich Fromm sighs that we have produced "men that act like machines and machines that act like men." Dr. Viktor Frankl of Vienna recently said, "Time and time again, the psychiatrist is consulted by patients who doubt that life has any meaning." Dr. Frankl calls this condition "existential vacuum" and reports that no less than 81 percent of his American students (as against 40 percent of the Europeans) say they have felt it.

Modern literature also testifies to this purposelessness. A hero to many of our students today is Holden Caulfield, central character in J. D. Salinger's *Catcher in the Rye*. Caulfield, on the verge of flunking out of his New England prep school, disappointed with his executive father and socialite mother, who have no time for him, and convinced that his teachers, the preachers, and all of society are "phonies," leaves school and takes off for New York City for a lost weekend. He tries to get drunk, but only succeeds in getting sick. He calls a prostitute to his room, but is so disgusted with himself that he can't go through with it. Finally he heads for home, his family's midtown apartment. On the way he crosses Central Park and hears some children singing an old Scottish folk song, "Coming through the Rye." At home he finds his seven-year-old sister, who in her childish simplicity seems to him to be the only real person in the world. He tries to tell her something of his experience and recounts the song the children were singing.

"If a body catch a body . . " he begins.

"No," corrects his sister. "It's if a body kiss a body."

Holden goes on to tell her that he likes to sing it "catch."

"I thought it was 'if a body catch a body,' " he said. "Anyway, I keep picturing all of these little kids playing some game in this big field of rye and all. Thousands of little kids, and nobody's around—nobody big, I mean—except me. And I'm standing on the edge of some crazy cliff. What I have to do, I have to catch everybody if they start to go over the cliff, I mean if they're running and they don't look where they're going, I have to come out from somewhere and catch them. That's all I do all day. I'd just be the catcher in the rye and all. I know it's crazy, but that's the only thing I'd really like to be. I know it's crazy."[7]

For all his cynicism, Holden Caulfield, and all the Holden Caulfields of the twentieth century, wonder if somewhere, someplace, there isn't something or someone worth committing themselves to.

This emptiness may prove to be our best point of contact for relevant evangelism today. I remember a young business executive in Oklahoma who described his pilgrimage to Christ. "I asked the older generation what I should live for," he mused, "and they in effect said, 'Seek ye first the vice-presidency and all things shall be added unto you.' But I looked at them, and many of them were vice-presidents, and they weren't happy." It was through this longing for real purpose that he and many of his peers found Christ.

How, then, are we to present the relevance of Christ for personal need? Certainly not as a Christ who is only a crutch for the maimed. Most assuredly not as a beggar Christ, seeking for man's condescending patronage. We shall present him as the Imperial Lord—"for we preach not ourselves, but Christ Jesus as Lord." We shall present him as Lord over death—"I am the resurrection and the life." We shall present him as Lord over sin and guilt—"I am come to give my life a ransom for many." We shall proclaim him as Lord over the meaningless—'I am the Way—follow me,' remembering that at the bottom it is not the fear that Christ is irrelevant that makes men turn from him. Rather, it is the knowledge that he is too relevant, too disturbing, too demanding. And it is only when men see his total Lordship, his claim to all of life, that they will see his relevancy as their Savior.

The Christian life must begin with personal experience, but it must not end there. If Jesus Christ is Lord of all, then he is Lord of our relationship to others in society. It is a scandal when we as Christ's disciples compartmentalize our lives, putting our personal piety in one segment and our social responsibility in another.

Think of John Campbell White, the Scottish chemical manufacturer, who was influenced by Moody to become an evangelical leader in missions, revival, Sabbath observance, and abstinence. What a scandal it was when Keir Hardie showed that White's employees were paid only three to four pence an hour, worked twelve hours a day with no time off for meals, had for the most part not one day off a week, and worked in horrid filth! White's defense was that he was so busy with his religious activities that he left the direction of his business to others!

White is not the norm. One need not search far through history to find the social impact of the Gospel—as in the abolition of slavery. "The two doctrines which contributed most to the abolition of slavery," declared Benjamin Kidd in his *Social Evolution*, "were the doctrine of salvation and the doctrine of the equality of all men before the Deity."[8]

John Howard, the great champion of prison reform, was quick to recognize John Wesley's influence on his life. "I was encouraged by him to go on vigorously with my own designs," he wrote of a meeting with Wesley in Dublin. "I saw in him how much a single man might achieve by zeal and perseverance; and I thought, why may I not do as much in my way as Mr. Wesley has done in his, if I am only as persevering? And I determined that I would pursue my work with more alacrity than ever."[9]

Like our Lord, who healed the sick and fed the hungry, we must see men as whole men, not as disembodied souls to be prepackaged for heaven. Evangelicals today must be deeply concerned to stand in the great tradition of those who down through the centuries have given the lie to the charge that we are simply promoting "pie in the sky."[10]

A lady heard Billy Graham speak to a large dinner meeting several years ago. Obviously captivated, she turned to Billy's wife, Ruth, and exclaimed, "Oh, I think he's wonderful! Isn't it too bad he's not in politics!" What shall we say to such folk?

We must say that Christian evangelism provides both a power and a perspective, the dynamism and the realism needed to confront our problems. First, the Christian Evangel provides a spiritual and moral dynamism. Recently, Dr. W. B. Harvey, former professor of political science at the University of Western Ontario, made a striking statement. "In mechanical advance," he said, "the essence of the problem is invention or discovery; the use or application of the invention is almost automatic. In moral, economic or political advance, the problem is to get people to act on a new or higher plane."

In Colombia I once discussed President Kennedy's Alliance for Progress with a South American newspaper editor. He pointed out that reforms could not be carried out there as simply as we in North America might imagine. There was the need to create a desire for self-betterment among the common people. I asked the editor, "Would it be fair to say that the most basic need in your country is a human revolution?" And he quickly nodded his agreement. In other words they needed a moral dynamism.

This is precisely what Jesus meant when he said two thousand years ago, "You must be born again." New technology without new men simply creates new and more fearsome problems. This is where the relevance—nay more, the absolute imperative—of conversion comes in. Conversion is the point where a man ceases to be so much of the problem and begins to be part of the solution.

Conversion brings, as we saw above, release from the anxiety about death. It is the fear of death that brings a basic insecurity to man, driving him into various pressure groups and power blocs. But when the eternal security of the love of God in Jesus Christ, from which nothing can separate us, breaks in upon a man, he finds his deep-rooted insecurity dispelled, and is in turn free to love, to understand, and to share with others.

Conversion means release from guilt, and this also is fraught with social significance. Guilt arises from a sense of inferiority and failure and always produces a reflex action of self-defense, and usually aggressiveness toward others. A father comes home from the office and lashes out at the children. Why? Because he doesn't like children? Not at all. He is venting his hostility because his boss criticized him at the office for something he did badly. These personal quarrels are simply war in miniature. Flash the pattern of a family feud on a universal screen and you have the microcosm of a world war!

We shall never deal ultimately with war and prejudice until we face this problem of guilt—until we see that while men do not want war, they want the things that cause war. Only at the cross can the walls of partition that fragment our world be effectively broken down.

Forgiveness involves a new attitude to others. "Forgive as God for Christ's sake has forgiven you." The man who has freely accepted the amazing grace of God will show it in a new selflessness toward others. One thinks of Jacob DeShazer, the Air Force crewman interned in Japan during World War II, who went back to that country after the war as a missionary to declare the reconciliation of Christ.

Conversion also produces a new sense of purpose. The convert has a new aim, to serve Jesus Christ as Lord and to further his purposes in all of life. This has great repercussions, for example, in today's search for freedom. Is it enough to be free from something? Must we not be free for something? "For what?" The Christian faith roots freedom solidly in the sovereignty of God, and sees it as freedom to serve and do his will. Humanism, on the other hand, sees freedom as human autonomy. Its moral relativism is an inadequate foundation, as shown in the fact that

Communism itself grew out of the humanistic tradition in the West. On what ground can the humanist consistently hold freedom to be more ideal than totalitarianism, while claiming his own personal preference as the ultimate authority? As John Shepard has pointed out, "Without the recognition of the authority of God as its basis, any concept of freedom is subject to relativism, and men turn away from freedom to some new authority."

Only the man who himself knows the experience of being set free to serve Christ can teach freedom to others. Witness William Wilberforce, self-seeking young playboy of his day, who—transformed by a conversion experience while on holiday in France—became, under God, the great emancipator of slaves. "You shall know the truth, and the truth shall make you free."

But the Christian Evangel provides more than a spiritual dynamism. It also offers a theological realism. This frame of reference is sorely needed by the social reformer, who faces the twin dangers of a false optimism or a false pessimism. The Christian is neither an optimist nor pessimist. He is a realist.

He is a realist because he takes seriously the fact of human sin. He does not fall easily into the idealistic fallacy of treating symptoms instead of causes, of supposing that with a little more literacy, food, shelter, recreation, and welfare benefit the millennium will arrive. He believes, as Reinhold Niebuhr put it, that "man's capacity for good makes democracy possible; but man's capacity for evil makes democracy necessary." He therefore takes politics and law seriously, believing that God in his grace has ordained these means of curbing the outbreaks of man's innate, sinful self-centeredness.

The idealist is always in great danger of swerving right across to bitter cynicism when he encounters the stony fact of human stubbornness, and sees his fondest plans shipwrecked on the jagged rocks of self-interest. But the Christian realist is prevented from falling into this abyss of pessimism. His motive in the first place is not success, but faithfulness to the command of Christ. He is not bound to "bring in the kingdom" and make the world over in this generation by his own power. He is bound to witness to the Lordship of Christ, and to seek the most concrete possible expressions of the love of Christ in his generation.

Philippe Maury expressed it well: "The Christian in politics will give himself wholly to the action in which he is engaged, yet remain skeptical about what he is doing. Success is not indispensable, because his final hope is not political but in the glory of God. Political action should be a means of making clear the meaning of faith in Christ."[11]

And this applies to all social action. Christian realism operates through faith working in love—and that faith is the substance of things hoped for. The Christian is not a man who expects to eliminate social evil totally from his world. But he does not refrain from doing anything just because he cannot do everything. He knows that the church cannot make all things perfect, but it can make some things better. He is committed in personal relations to express the redeeming love of Christ to his neighbor; and he is committed in social situations to express that love through social justice. He will work for "contingent solutions"—limited and precarious as they may be, never satisfied with the partial good and yet never losing heart, because he sees by faith "new heavens and a new earth, wherein dwelleth righteousness."

It is the triumphant return of Christ at the end of history that brings hope to this Christian realism. The Christian is like a man who has read the last chapter of a novel. He knows where the plot is going to end, though he may not guess the heartaches and tragedies that lie in the intervening chapters. He knows where history is going, for he knows where Christ is going.

But is it enough for us to point to historical illustrations and theological systems? Are we prepared personally to pay the price of involvement? Where are our Wilberforces and Howards today? Where are the men and women who will not only say that Christ is relevant, but demonstrate his relevancy in our burning contemporary problems?

How, for example, would Christian dynamism and Christian realism operate in terms of two of our greatest problems: war and race?

Christians have long debated about war, some in terms of the just war, some upholding pacifism. The problem is severely complicated today by the emergence of nuclear weapons capable of destroying great segments of innocent civilian populations. As one who would believe there can be "just war," I still tremble at the thought of nuclear weapons being used to wipe out whole cities.

As nuclear weapons proliferate among more nations, does the idea of "nuclear deterrent" not lose its credibility? Can nations reasonably expect to use tactical low-yield nuclear weapons and still stop escalation into all-out warfare? And is there a point where the worldwide devastation of such an all-out nuclear conflict makes nonsense of "fighting to preserve freedom," because there would be no societies left to be free? These are hard questions to which the experts seek hard answers. The Christian has no monopoly on wisdom here. It seems to me that Christian realism should press for disarmament with safeguards, and an international police force with teeth. Yet Christian dynamism should not be satisfied to stop there. It should insist that we use the breathing spell created by these deterrents for an all-out evangelistic push into the materially and spiritually underprivileged areas of the world, to teach the illiterate, feed the hungry, heal the sick, and preach the Gospel of reconciliation.

The matter of race relations is one in which the church has too long defaulted. Many say, "You cannot make men love by law." That is quite true. But Christian realism is not content with this, for it knows that love in social terms is expressed in justice for all races and minorities. I admired the candor of a young Birmingham, Alabama, teenager who appeared some time ago on a TV program discussing race relations in her city. "I realize," she admitted, "that I need law to make me do what I ought to do but don't want to do." But again Christian dynamism is never satisfied with deeds. It thinks in terms of motives. It seeks a community of reconciliation where men will not only do right, but want the right. Its standard is "Thou shalt love thy neighbor as thyself." Therefore, it will seek opportunity to proclaim that by faith "we are all one in Christ Jesus."

There was a man in Richmond, Virginia, who had been asked to serve as an ushering captain during the Billy Graham Crusade in that city. When he heard that Negroes and whites were to attend and sit together just as they pleased, he tore off his badge and resigned in hot fury. A few nights later, he came to the ushering assignment table and asked for his badge back. He explained that in the interval he had come to the Crusade meetings, heard the Gospel, been converted, and now had a new attitude to all his brethren regardless of the color of their skin!

It is time that many of our Christian churches began to pioneer in bridging the racial gap between churches. One exciting experiment is the so-called "exchange program" in which a Negro and a white church will designate three or four families each to attend and work in the other church for a limited period of, say, three months, to be followed by repeated series of exchanges until the two congregations have come to know each other in a new way.

We must never forget that the God who redeemed us is the God who created us and is concerned for all of life. We must constantly affirm that the Christ who died for us is the Christ who was incarnate in human flesh and involved in our human situation. We must be willing to take a towel, as he did, and wash dirty feet if we would proclaim Jesus Christ as Lord and ourselves men's servants for his sake.

We know that Jesus Christ is relevant to this burdened, bleeding, broken world. The point is that Christ wants to use us to show the world that he is relevant, that he does matter to them, and that they do matter to him. He has given to us this ministry of reconciliation. In the year 1909, the Hon. Earl Balfour was lecturing at the University of Edinburgh on "The Moral Values Which Unite Nations." He had mentioned diplomatic contacts, commerce, common knowledge, common friendships. At the end there was applause and a question period. Then a Japanese student rose and asked, "But, Mr. Balfour, what about Jesus Christ?" There was dead silence. Everybody felt the irony of the question as a foreign student from a far-off non-Christian land inquired of one of the great diplomatic leaders of the greatest Christian nation of that day, "What about Jesus Christ?"

This is how we make evangelism relevant. We ask of a world wistfully searching for security, forgiveness, purpose, peace, and love, "What about Jesus Christ?"

[1]W.E. Sangster, *Let Me Commend* (London: The Epworth Press, 1961), p. 10.

[2]William Barclay, *The Gospel of John, Vol. I, The Daily Study Bible Series* (Edinburgh: The Saint Andrew Press, 1955), p. 209.

[3]Douglas Webster, *What Is Evangelism?* (London: The Highway Press, 1959), Chap. 2. I am indebted for much of the discussion which immediately follows to Canon Webster's excellent analysis.

[4]John Osborne, *Look Back in Anger*, (Great Meadows, N. J.: S. G. Phillips, Inc., 1957).

[5]Dietrich Bonhoeffer, *Letters and Papers from Prison* (London: S.C.M. Press, 1953), pp. 145 f.

[6]Donald Baillie, *God Was in Christ* (London: Faber & Faber, 1948), p. 166.

[7]J.D. Salinger, *Catcher in the Rye* (New York: Signet Books, 1953), p. 156.

[8]Quoted in A. Skevington Wood, *The Inextinguishable Blaze* (London: The Paternoster Press, 1960), p. 244.

[9]*Ibid.*, p. 246.

[10]The verdict of the distinguished church historian, F. J. Foakes-Jackson, is worth noting. "History shows that the thought of Christ on the Cross has been more potent than anything else in arousing a compassion for suffering and indignation at injustice . . . The later Evangelicalism, which saw in the death of Christ the means of free salvation for fallen humanity, caused its adherents to take the front rank as champions of the weak . . . Prison reform, the prohibition of the slave trade, the abolition of slavery, the Factory Acts, the protection of children, the crusade against cruelty to animals, are all the outcome of the great Evangelical revival of the eighteenth century." F. J. Foakes-Jackson, "Christ in the Church: The Testimony of History," in H. B. Swete, *Cambridge Theological Essays* (New York: The Macmillan Company, 1905), pp. 512 ff.

[11]Quoted in the *Christian Century*, Mar. 16, 1949, p. 347.